BUSINESS STRATEGY & PLANNING

Edited by Bernard Taylor

Hazards of growth
How to succeed through company planning

Bruno Hake
English version by Peter Gray Lucas

Longman

LONGMAN GROUP LIMITED
London
Associated companies, branches and representatives throughout the world

Original German edition (published as *Wachstum Sinnvoll Planen* by Econ Verlag, Düsseldorf)
© Bruno Hake 1971

English version © Longman Group Ltd. 1974.
All rights reserved. No part of this publication may be reproduced, stored in a retrieval system, or transmitted in any form or by any means, electronic, mechanical, photocopying, recording, or otherwise, without the prior permission of the Copyright owner.

English translation first published 1974

ISBN 0582 45020 9

Library of Congress Catalog Card Number: 73-86112

Set in 11 point Joanna type
and printed in Great Britain
by Cox & Wyman Ltd,
London, Fakenham and Reading

Contents

	PREFACE	Page vii
1	Introduction	1
2	Basic principles of company planning	4
3	The company appraisal	14
4	Formulating the company objectives	27
5	Market planning	34
6	Diversification as a marketing strategy	53
7	Ways of implementing an expansion programme	64
8	Financial planning	78
9	The strategy of conglomerates	89
10	Product planning	92
11	Weakness of futurology and market research for company planning	99
12	Manpower planning	102
13	Organisation planning in the growing firm	110
14	The organisation of company planning	119
	APPENDIX: The Checklists	127
	INDEX OF NAMES AND PRODUCTS	155

Checklists and Examples

Checklists

1	The process of integrated company planning	13,	129
2	The company appraisal: Part 1 The current situation	25,	131
	The company appraisal: Part 2 Future developments	26,	133
3	Quantitative planning objectives	33,	135
4	Rationalisation methods	37,	137
5	Market research	39,	139
6	Market planning	40,	141

7 Licensing contracts	69–70,	143–4
8 Product planning	98,	145
9 The personnel manager's duties	109,	147
10 The company planner's responsibilities	121,	149
11 Common reasons for the failure of company planning	122,	151
12 The planning consultant's brief	125,	153

Examples

MARKET PLANNING

1 A manufacturer of construction equipment, 1973–8
 Part 1 Alternative market strategies   45
 Part 2 Choosing between alternative market strategies   46–7
 Part 3 Action programme for 1973   48
2 A manufacturer of sunglasses, 1973–78
 Part 1 Alternative market strategies   49
 Part 2 Choosing between alternative market strategies   50–1
 Part 3 Action programme for 1973   52

MANPOWER PLANNING

3 Calculation of labour turnover   105
4 Calculation of staff needed for the expansion of the sales force   105

Preface

What must a company do to survive the hazards of growth and prosper in a fast-expanding economy?

On the continent of Europe and in the USA many firms have been learning the hard way. They have already had the kind of experience that British companies will be living through in the next few years as our own rate of growth increases. This book is a practical record of the lessons that have been learned.

Many familiar names of companies that managed to learn the lessons quickly and survived are mentioned here. Some unfamiliar names are also mentioned: they were the firms that did not learn in time. British managers need not repeat their mistakes.

The basic message is simple. A faster rate of growth in a much larger economic community means in practice a greatly heightened rate of change. Individual firms will indeed have new opportunities to grow in size and profitability, but they will have to operate in a much more rapidly changing economic environment. From the individual firm's point of view change is a random process: it may be lucky, neutral or unlucky in its effects. The counter-measure to more rapid change is more and better planning.

'Planning' is a word that is sometimes atrociously misconstrued. What Mr Hake means by planning is doing the preparatory work now for decisions that will have to be taken next year and the year after, instead of allowing the future of the company to be determined by the cumulative effect of disconnected day-to-day decisions. Planning does NOT mean formulating long term schemes that are supposed to guide the company towards grandiose objectives regardless of the turbulence around it.

Planning starts with managers thinking much harder than they have been accustomed to, about all aspects of the company's PRESENT situation. After a careful appraisal of present strengths and weaknesses, provisional objectives are formulated that look generally sensible and feasible. The provisional objectives are then tested by working out in detail exactly how, by what steps, the company could proceed towards them from its present position. If some of the steps prove on closer inspection to be impracticable, the objectives are modified.

Gradually a coherent and practicable set of plans comes to light.

As time goes by, the achievement within the company is monitored step by step and the environment is monitored for unexpected opportunities and threats. The company may still be caught out by completely unforeseeable changes, but at least it will not have been caught napping.

In rendering Mr Hake's book into English we have used the term 'company planning' in preference to the term 'corporate planning' that is currently in fashion in the academic literature. It is not just the large corporation that needs to plan. The small or medium company is in fact more acutely threatened by change, but is also in a better position to make a quick response to change. The quick response can only be an effective one if the company knows clearly where it is – or was – going and can recognise, well in advance of the event, where its path is getting unexpectedly blocked and where a new path is suddenly opening up.

This book tells you how to do it. What company planning means in practice is that managers have to ask themselves a lot more questions. The answers are of course different for every firm, but the questions are much the same for most firms in manufacturing, trading and service industries. The general policy questions that the management will have to ask itself, collectively and individually for the various functional areas, will be found in the text. The detailed questions that will elicit the required data and form the specific operating decisions will be found in CHECKLISTS which appear in the appropriate chapters and are repeated in the Appendix at the end of the book. Readers may find it convenient to detach the extra copy of a Checklist and take it away to work on. This can be done without mutilating the body of the book.

The questions are illustrated by copious practical examples. This is a most unusual book on management, in that at least as much space is given to illustrating how things went wrong as is given to the successes of planning. Evidently it is very far from being a book by a theoretical expert about yet another management technique that is going to solve all the company's problems.

As Chairman of a School of Management devoted exclusively to helping practising managers to improve their performance on the job, I can commend Mr Hake's book wholeheartedly to English-speaking managers. I believe they will find it helpful, and I am quite sure they will not find it dull.

The Hatfield Polytechnic School of Management, P. GRAY LUCAS
Hatfield, Herts Chairman,
July 1973.

1

Introduction

The only constant thing is change. This was said by a Greek philosopher, and it will be even more true in the future than in the past. In the 1970s the tempo of economic, social, technical and political change will be faster than ever before.

This will bring both opportunities and dangers for the firm. Turnover and profits can only be substantially increased if the opportunities for future change are recognised in good time and exploited to the full. If threatening dangers are not recognised and averted by suitable measures, loss of markets, profits and assets can happen with unexpected rapidity.

An investment that looks right in today's conditions can turn out to be wrong in a very few years' time. Managers will need to be better aware of economic, social and technical developments than they have been in the past, and will have to take them into account in all their plans for the future.

The more persistent the process of change, the more powerful are the future effects of today's actions, and the easier it is for today's wrong decisions or 'sins of omission' to have become burdens on the firm by tomorrow. Hence, **long-term planning has become the most important task of the senior executive** – and by planning we mean doing the preparatory work now for decisions that will have to be taken at some future time. Long-term company planning means that what the company is going to do in the areas of sales, finance, product development, investment, production and manpower over the next five to ten years is planned in broad outline now, taking account of economic, technical, social and political changes over the same period in so far as they can be foreseen. The purpose of long-term company planning is to display to the manager in good time what the possibilities are, so that he can take his decisions on the basis of well-established facts.

The future of the company thus moves to the centre of the planning process. The answer to the question 'where will the company stand in ten years' time?' is not left to the cumulative effect of day-to-day decisions, but is the outcome of coordinated long-term measures.

Company planning does not mean abolishing the need for initiative in particular parts of the firm, and does not mean 'levelling-down'. Nor does its successful implementation require the gift of clairvoyance.

Why should the company executive concern himself with planning for the future? Because it forces him to proceed methodically and makes it easier for him to shape the future of the company according to his own idea of its objectives.

Obviously not every plan can be implemented. Even if a carefully worked out plan looks feasible at present, there is always the possibility of completely unforeseeable economic developments that may frustrate it.

The practical benefits of long-term planning are:

- It helps to reduce risks, because an attempt is made to work out how all the developments that are at present foreseeable will affect the firm, and to take account of these effects.
- It helps to ensure that opportunities are fully exploited, because they are recognised early and the necessary measures can be introduced in good time.
- It offers a strong incentive to the management to make greater efforts to reach the agreed objectives and to overcome difficulties that stand in the way.

These advantages are so weighty that the cost of company planning in time and money is always justified. It has been demonstrated in practice to be an effective management tool, but its application has been confined until now to a few large firms.

It is easy to justify a policy of doing nothing by saying 'Let's wait until the present uncertainties have been resolved'. People forget that the present uncertainties are always succeeded by others and that there will never be a time when planning can be done without any uncertainties at all.

The future will bring more rapid change in technology and in markets and, hence, more severe competition. Security is only for the company that plans and acts systematically. Even medium-sized firms will not survive without forward-looking and broadly-based planning. What has only recently been accepted by large firms will very soon be a condition of survival for medium-sized firms: only the firm that knows today exactly where it is going to stand in five years' and ten years' time has a good chance of being able to reach its objectives and withstand the competition.

It is no longer good enough to leave the future well-being of the company to fate or improvisation. Experience shows that there are **three main causes of lack of planning** or incomplete planning:

1 The study of practical problems and methods of company management is seldom fostered in European universities. Very few students of industrial economics have the opportunity to learn about company planning during their studies.
2 Company planning, like many other new methods, has become loaded with

Introduction

jargon and has thereby gained the reputation of being a science that is only open to specialists.
3 Many executives are so overburdened with day-to-day problems that they do not have time for the important but apparently not so urgent task of company planning: all the more so if it appears to them to be a secret science that they have to learn before they can make a start.

The purpose of this book is to present the objectives and methods of company planning in an easily intelligible form, and to show how it can be used to bring about planned growth.

2

Basic principles of company planning

The purpose of company planning is to create the conditions today for the company to become aware of future market opportunities and to avoid dangers. It is therefore concerned with **four questions:**

1 Where does the company stand now?
2 What are its goals for the future?
3 How is its objective to be reached?
4 What decisions must be made now?

Company planning thus takes place in **four phases:**

1 Appraising the present situation, i.e. systematically investigating all the internal and external circumstances relevant to the future survival of the firm.
2 Setting the business objectives of the firm.
3 Deciding on the most favourable strategy for achieving these objectives, by critically examining the strategies that are in principle possible, and choosing the most favourable out of a number of possibilities.
4 Working out the plan of action for the current year and coordinating all sections of the firm, in order to implement the chosen strategy. Every section of the firm must be told what it will have to do if the company objectives are to be achieved.

In order to ensure that the company plan covers all the complex operations of the firm as a whole, the firm has to be divided into separate **planning areas,** namely:

- The marketing plan.
- The financial plan.
- The product development plan.
- The production plan.
- The organisation plan.
- The manpower plan.

The individual plans must be harmonised with each other to form the company plan. In this the coordinating role is played by the financial plan. Financial planning does not mean projecting bookkeeping figures into the future. It means checking the effects of the individual plans on returns, liquidity and the need for capital and working out the financial measures that will be required in the future, such as the provision of new capital.

Bringing together the individual plans to form a company plan is known as *integrated planning*. It is naturally a larger and more costly undertaking than confining the planning operation to one or two separate plans, such as the marketing plan or the production plan.

If the separate plans can be properly coordinated, the planning as a whole becomes more realistic and more effective. Furthermore, the mistakes are avoided that might arise from not paying proper regard to certain aspects of the firm's operations.

Planning in limited areas only, without making full use of the financial plan to coordinate the other plans, is known as *open planning*.

Open planning is simpler and costs less in time and money. Firms that are embarking on long-term planning are therefore recommended first to build up an open planning system, and only to attempt to go over to integrated planning after several years' practical experience of partial company planning. However, an open planning system should always include financial planning as well as market and production planning, as a safeguard against unpleasant surprises, such as running out of cash.

Market planning and financial planning are the key to company planning

Market planning and financial planning occupy the central position in any planning system, because:

- The market decides whether the firm has the chance to grow or whether it is exposed to the dangers of falling demand or increasing competition: market planning has the job of working out how far the objectives of the firm can be achieved within its traditional markets and how much penetration of new markets (diversification) will be needed.
- Financial planning has the job of checking whether the separate market, product development, production, manpower and organisation plans will bring an adequate return, and whether the financial resources that will be needed for the realisation of the detailed plans can be made available.

The market situation is the basis for all the separate plans, which, in turn, have to be integrated by the financial plan. In effect, checking profitability and establishing that the necessary resources can be provided is the decisive constraint on all detailed plans.

Company planning without the key areas of market and financial planning would be meaningless. But long-term planning is not absolutely necessary in all the other areas, although the company will only reap the full benefit when all areas have been integrated.

In practice, many firms plan the expansion of their production facilities several years in advance – they usually have to, because of the time it takes to acquire land and to obtain delivery of machines – but they do it without concerning themselves at the same time with market planning or financial planning.

An inquiry in Germany in the mid-1960s showed that less than 10 per cent of the industrial firms that were contacted practised any kind of medium- or long-term planning – and of these, 60 per cent concerned themselves with production planning alone. But what is the use of planning the production capacity for 1976 in the year 1973 without any security for financing it or selling the output? Production planning in isolation can only be regarded as technical construction, not as company planning.

The company must decide on the appropriate planning timespan

Company planning is usually concerned with developments over the next five to seven years. The most useful timespan to adopt depends to a substantial degree on the product life cycle of the particular firm and on the number of years over which its investments have to be written off.

When a chain of grocery stores plans a new discount store, it is putting capital into a fixed asset for ten to twenty years. It ought therefore to consider the likely population changes in its market area and the changes in their purchasing habits over a similar period, in so far as this is possible. In addition, the effect of the investment in a new discount store on the cash position of the firm and on other expansion plans (for example, extending the main store in the city centre) should also be worked out.

A manufacturer of fashion-wear, who can alter his production facilities and install new capacity within a period of one to two years, would be adequately served by a shorter planning timespan of two to four years.

A forecast for more than seven years ahead is capable neither of making reliable statements about future political and economic conditions, nor of generating data in sufficient detail to be used as a basis for the development of the firm and its relations with the market. If planning is attempted beyond this, it can only be in broad outlines. The term 'planning perspectives' is then appropriate.

Short-term and long-term planning must be coordinated

Company planning is often contrasted with short-term business planning. This shows a defective understanding of what planning is about. It is **not** the purpose to decide now, in 1973, what the firm will be doing in 1978. The purpose of planning is to investigate the measures that have to be taken today, so that the firm will find itself in the best position to operate successfully in the circumstances than can be expected in 1978. The manager can only act in the present. Company planning indicates to him what he must do at the present time in order to reach his future goals.

The timing of decisions is usually very important. Planning ensures not only that the right decisions are taken, but that they are taken early enough, and implemented.

The purpose of company planning is to provide the management with a concrete basis for translating global long-term targets into detailed objectives, and for reaching these objectives step by step through day to day operations.

Thus, there is no opposition in principle between long-, medium-, and short-term planning. The output from long-term planning is an action plan which is short-term in nature, and says what has to be done today.

Company planning is more than a piece of paper

The central importance of the annual action plan as the output from company planning is often misunderstood. Instead, the view may be taken that a formally written and carefully documented company plan is the first objective of planning. Formal questions of presentation should not be overemphasised. Inflexible models and formulae should be used with caution. Company planning is not 'art for art's sake'. Much more important than written presentation is the mastering and utilisation of the planning process in an organised and methodical way as a management tool. Only then can usable criteria for planning and decision making be given to the management centres responsible for carrying out the action plan. Planning is not a piece of paper, it cannot alone bring any improvement in turnover or profit. This comes about through well-directed measures taken on the basis of action plans. Good planning can only manifest itself in the form of purposeful action.

Planning is a continuous task

Company planning is both a continuous and an occasional task. Only through regular revision of the external and internal data can adaptations be made in the environment or in the company objectives that were not originally envisaged. At the same time, sudden changes of plan will occasionally be forced on the company by unexpected events. When this happens, new strategies and new action plans for implementing the company's objectives have to be worked out.

The plan must be controlled

Prompt control of the plan is vital, to ensure that the planning is changed quickly when changes are necessary. Regular comparisons of planned and actual results must be carried out. These comparisons represent the monitoring of the plan. The planning estimates for turnover, costs and profits must be compared at regular intervals with actual figures, and the causes of the variances investigated.

The rolling plan is the link between planning and budgeting

The planning timespan is divided into planning periods. A planning period of a year is usually adopted and has been shown to be adequate. In this way, turnover figures and financial and accounting data can be used for monitoring the plan without the need for complicated re-calculations.

A five-year period is usually long enough for company planning, and the budget for next year forms the first period. Each year the budget for the current year is taken out of the plan and a new period added at the front end.

While this is being done the intervening planning periods are reviewed and any necessary changes are carried out. Thus the five-year plan is implemented a year at a time, while the timespan remains constant. This is known as a 'rolling plan'.

The individual planning periods are not all worked out to the same degree of fine detail. Fully detailed planning should be confined to those parts of the plan that require decisions to be taken now. This implies that the action plans for the year immediately ahead are worked out in considerably more detail than those for two to five years ahead.

Monthly performance checks are an essential management tool

The output from company planning is the action plan, which shows what objectives have to be reached in the coming year, and what tasks have to be given to the individual line management centres.

The total annual plan is divided into sales, costs, capital investment and financial budgets. The estimates in the sales budget, for example, show the planned revenue by months, regions and product groups.

Actual and estimated sales figures can be compared. These comparisons should be made monthly, by regions and products. They are an admirable control instrument. Disturbances are shown up immediately, and the management can concentrate its attention on removing them. For example, it can consider in good time whether sales that have fallen below the planned figures can be brought back into line by special sales promotion measures, more frequent calls by sales representatives, or by other means.

Cost comparisons can be made in a similar way. It is important that costs should be analysed in terms of the cost centres responsible for incurring them. Monthly comparisons between estimated and actual costs act as a management control, and also serve to enhance the cost-consciousness of the management.

It is sufficient for control purposes to make monthly comparisons of only those costs that can be influenced in the short term. In this way, the attention of the employee is concentrated on those costs that he can actually influence. For instance, there is no point in including the monthly rent for a sales office occupied on a long lease in a monthly cost comparison, because nothing can be done about it in the short term; telephone and mileage expenses, however, can reasonably be checked monthly.

The benefits from comparisons between planned and actual figures can only be achieved in practice if the comparison is available promptly. Thus, the comparative figures for June should be available to all the departments concerned by 10 July. Costs go stale as fast as bread! If the June figures are not available until August or even September, they have lost their urgency. It is by then difficult to discover the causes of variances, and, above all, employees will not bother about 'out-of-date figures'.

It is therefore important to confine the monthly comparisons to a small number of relevant and easily understood figures, instead of striving after a fully detailed budgetary control in perfect accord with the best accounting theory.

The author's experience has repeatedly confirmed that an annual plan with individual budgets and monthly comparisons between budget and actual figures is a uniquely effective tool for management control of the firm.

Successful company planning is based on the annual plan

There are a number of firms that have an impressive long-term planning organisation, because that counts as being progressive, but have no annual plans and no monthly budgets.

These firms may announce proudly that they are going to double their turnover in five years' time, but they desist from deciding at the beginning of 1973 how much the sales representative Miller is going to sell in the Manchester sales district in June 1973. Hence, they are not in a position to worry about whether Mr Miller reached this sales figure in June or not. This is putting the cart before the horse.

Success in 1978 rests on the results for 1973, and the 1973 results are made up of a host of detailed results in particular months, regions and product groups. Only by getting a grip on these detailed results is it possible to influence the total results for 1978.

Only if the insights gained through company planning are applied in the form of action plans and budgets can the planning be effective. Only actions bring results. We can plan for the year 1978, but we can only act today.

To build up a budgeting system and to collect enough practical experience to operate it successfully takes at least two or three years. A great deal of time and work has to be put in before monthly comparisons of sales, costs and financial figures can be made into a useful management tool. The time and effort is inescapable if an effective company planning system is to be constructed.

An effectively operating annual financial budget is an equally important prerequisite for successful long-term investment planning. Only if the firm knows what money it is going to need in the current year is there any point at all in doing it. All capital investment should therefore be preplanned in the annual budget, and there must be an authorisation procedure to ensure that no money is spent on capital investment that has not been budgeted. This is how company planning must be interlocked with annual budget planning. If this is not done, company planning will be sterile: it will be nothing but a piece of paper.

Company planning plays only an advisory role with respect to the compilation of the annual plan detailing the measures to be implemented in the short term. The detailed plans for the coming year must be worked out by the managers in charge of the appropriate line management centres. The Sales Manager, for example, will be working out in 1973 his marketing plan and sales budget for 1974, taking into consideration the plans worked out by the company planning staff. This sales budget will then be presented to the Board for approval.

The plan must be adapted when circumstances change

If the sales plan departs from the sales target that has been set for 1974 in the company plan, the following possibilities are open to the top executive:

1 The Sales Manager can be asked to make a new marketing plan and a new sales budget, in order to try to match the target for 1974. He must, however, be willing to take responsibility for the new budget, and not regard it as a piece of homework to which he is not personally committed.
2 If it is concluded that the original target for 1974 is no longer realistic, the management must check whether the departure from the plan is attributable to special factors which will not recur (for example, a temporary setback in the general economy, the loss of a sales representative, or special activities of competitors) or whether a basic mismatch between the company plan and actuality exists.
3 If there are special factors, it may suffice for the management to take special compensatory action, such as appointing a new sales representative, starting a special sales promotion of its own, etc. The company plan will then not need to be altered fundamentally.
4 If there are fundamental differences between the assumptions underlying the

company plan and the facts of the market, the plan must be checked for mistakes. Alternatives have to be worked out which take account of the changed circumstances, but still make it possible to achieve the company objectives. An attempt is then made to alter the operational plans without giving up the company objectives.

5 If after critical examination of the new alternatives it is decided that the original company objectives cannot be achieved, then these objectives must be corrected.

This should make it clear that neither the plans nor the objectives of the company are fixed by company planning absolutely. Company planning must be flexible, not only to accommodate unexpected difficulties, but to make the most of unexpected opportunities, so long as they can be fitted into the overall objectives of the company. For example, the opportunity may arise suddenly to buy another company or to get into an interesting new market. In such cases, it may be better to exploit these possibilities – after carefully checking all their advantages and disadvantages and their consequences for the company objectives – rather than obstinately to stick to the course already laid down.

Company planning is a communication problem

The firm must not constrict itself by its own planning. But company planning must be taken seriously and not regarded as a theoretical exercise. To fulfil this requirement, it must not only be realistic, but it must be accepted by line management. This gives rise to serious communication problems, over which many company plans and company planners have come to grief. The company planner has got to *sell* his plan.

Planning has to be sold not only to the top executives, but to the line managers in the fields of sales, product development, production, organisation and finance. The best way of doing this is to let them participate in the planning.

Company planning demands a suitable management style

Planning has not been carried out properly if only one possible way of achieving the company objectives has been investigated. Several ideas must be developed, tested for their feasibility, their advantages and disadvantages displayed, and finally put before the management for selection of the best.

Company planning therefore has both pragmatic and systematic features. It is born of a management style that embraces the systematic preparation of decisions and the use of decision techniques. It is pragmatic, in that it does not suppose that to reach a goal or to solve a problem there is a single optimum path that can be discovered by scientific methods. But neither is it intuitive: it does not try to follow a path chosen on accidental, historical or personal grounds alone. Nevertheless, it is systematic in its technique for taking decisions, because it uses an analytical procedure, which consists of the following steps:

- Setting the operation's objectives.
- Identifying the existing problems.
- Working out a considerable number of solutions that are possible in principle (so-called alternatives).
- Determining the advantages and disadvantages of each possibility with respect to the difficulties of implementing it and its contribution to company objectives.
- Choosing the most favourable alternative for the particular company by the application of objective criteria.

Company planning can become a useful tool in the framework of this management style, but, in practice, a lengthy period of 'education' is often necessary. One cannot expect that a company that has been working on the principle of 'management by intuition' can suddenly switch to making full use of company planning. The hope of finding in company planning a 'scientific' and therefore infallible instrument is equally vain.

Company planning helps to improve the quality of decision techniques used in management; decisions become more lucid and the grounds of the decisions more secure. It enables the manager to recognise the range of choices that are open to him and thereby increases his freedom of action. Through company planning management becomes a more objective activity. Company planning has a strongly rationalising influence. Its costs are small in comparison with its benefits.

The practical process of introducing company planning in a real-life firm demands time and patience. As we have seen, considerable changes in attitudes and in management methods may have to be introduced before planning can begin to have a real effect on turnover, projects and growth. Compromises have to be accepted and the logical order of events may have to be modified in order to avoid holding up the whole development because of some intractable difficulty.

It is all the more important, therefore, that all concerned should have a clear picture of the logical stages of company planning, as shown on page 13, so that everyone is clear what part of the process they are working on at any given time, even if the parts have to be taken out of order.

Checklist 1 The process of integrated company planning

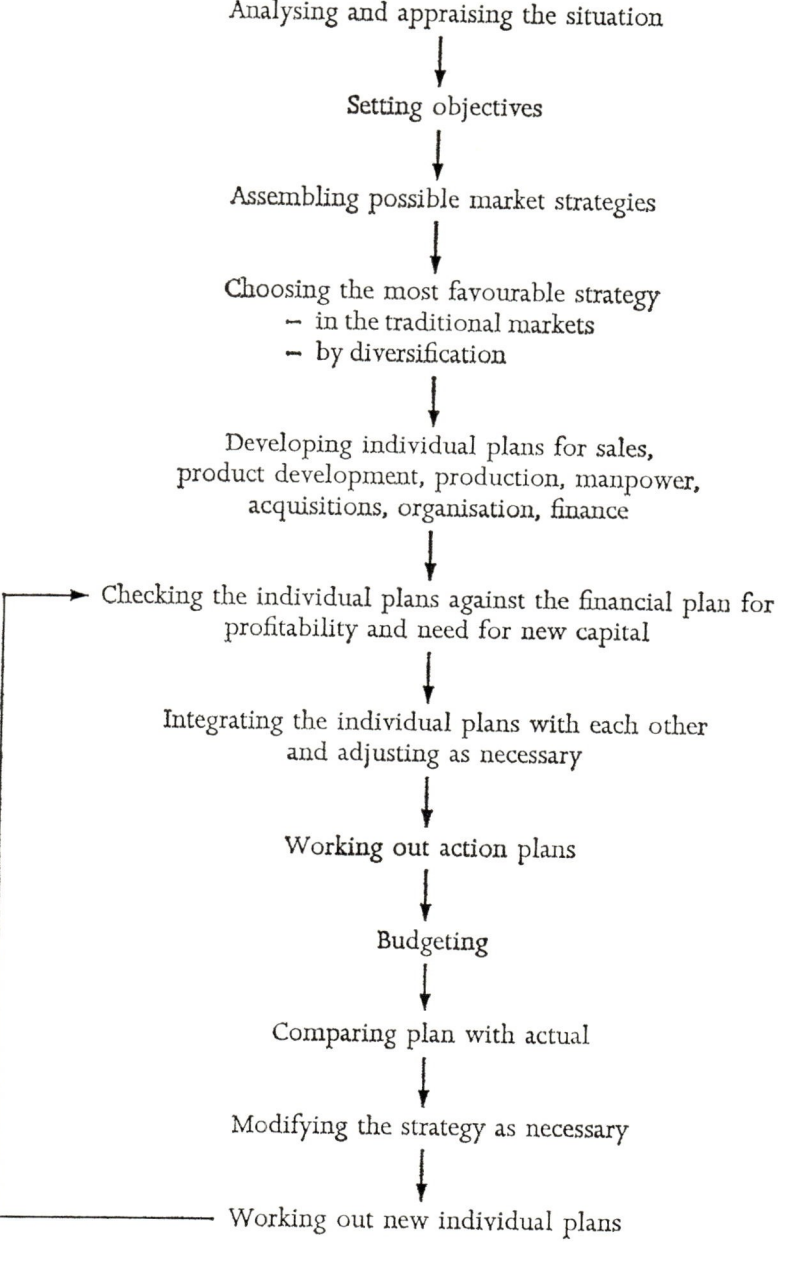

3

The company appraisal

The purpose of a company appraisal is to lay bare the present situation and capacity of the company and its future position in its area of activity. The **question** to be answered is:

- Where does the company stand now?

The company appraisal serves to establish the initial conditions for the later sections of the planning process. It is the foundation of the whole process of company planning. Mistakes and omissions made at this stage can have particularly serious consequences for the results of planning and for the future of the company. The appraisal therefore deserves to be handled with special care.

It should not be confined to critical appraisal of the internal capacity in the areas of development, production and sales. In order to appraise the company's future standing in its area of activity, it is necessary to identify the likely development of the market and to investigate whether the company will be able to maintain itself under changed market conditions. Only when these problems have been clarified is there any sense in considering new market strategies, such as diversification, in the later stages of planning.

The company appraisal covers the following **problem areas**:

- The company's products and the customers' appraisal of them.
- The capability of the sales organisation.
- The production facilities, reviewed from the point of view of technological status and economic viability.
- The future development of the market with respect to the market size, the technical demands on the product, the structure of the customers, the sales channels, and the competition.
- The capability of the company for adapting its products and its selling methods to the future demands of the market.

The current position of the firm in its market must be appraised

The current situation in the areas of manpower and finance is best taken up in the process of manpower and financial planning. This chapter is therefore mainly concerned with the company appraisal as a preparation for market planning. The list of topics makes it clear that a large part of the information required for a company appraisal has to be obtained by market research.

In practice, it is advisable to take the company appraisal in **two stages**:

1 The current standing of the firm in its market.
2 The future development of the market, with special regard to the technical demands on the product, the development of sales channels, and the size of the market.

This is the only way of making a correct assessment of the future position of the firm in relation to its market. It is a matter of decisive importance for the later stages of planning to know whether the firm can maintain or even improve its position in its present market or whether it must undertake a planned withdrawal in order to go into more promising markets.

A checklist of questions to be asked about the current situation and future developments appears on pages 25 and 26.

The current position of the firm in its market must be appraised

In the first stage the present situation of the firm is subjected to a critical appraisal. What is the capability of the firm in the area of production, development and sales? Are the demands of the market on products, sales organisation and customer service being satisfied? Are the employees satisfying the demands made on them? The firm should look at itself not only from inside, but also from outside, that is, through the eyes of the customers.

Thus the judgment of the firm, its products and its sales organisation, formed by its customers and trading partners, deserves to be treated with special respect.

There are two **yardsticks** that can be applied:

1 Comparison of the performance of the firm with that of its competitors.
2 Comparison with the expectations and judgments of the customers.

Under the first heading, a manufacturer of washing machines might discover that his three leading competitors had thirty to forty customer service stations, whereas he had only ten. Under the second heading, the importance of this finding might be confirmed if the outcome of an inquiry among customers was 'unsatisfactory customer service'.

Discovering the 'image' of the firm among its actual and potential customers forms an important part of the appraisal.

In consumer goods, especially, the firm's image plays a decisive part in company planning. Different departmental stores, such as Harrods, Selfridges and John Lewis, have very different images and, therefore, different bodies of regular customers. Their starting positions for taking, for example, a high-class line of fashion-wear into their ranges are quite different. The consumers' judgment and the firm's image can, of course, be altered by intensive advertising and public relations effort. But, in order to plan such measures, the judgments of the consumers about the particular firm and its competitors, as well as the reasons for these judgments, must be known. It may only be possible to make a reasoned choice between alternative market strategies if the firm has detailed knowledge about its image.

The consequences of future market changes must be investigated

For the second stage of its appraisal of itself, the firm needs to know as much as possible about future market developments. The qualitative aspects, as well as the questions of future market potential, deserve special attention. Market researchers are inclined to concern themselves too exclusively with developments in the size of the market: 'the market for machine tools will grow by 40 per cent in the next five years'. But for the company planner the following qualitative questions about **changes in the nature of the market** are also of decisive importance:

- How will the demands of the customers or the efforts of competitors affect the technical characteristics of the products in the future?
- How will the composition of the customers and the structure of the trade change in the future? Which sales channels will increase in importance and what consequences will this have for the sales effort and the market standing of the firm?

In **appraising market changes,** the company planner must ask himself the question:

- Is the company in a position to satisfy the customers' demands under the new market conditions, while continuing to trade profitably?

Sales can fall off for reasons other than an overall decline in demand or an increase in competition. The firm's future position may be weakened because of being unable to satisfy the new demands of the market. For example, the trend towards high performance machine tools with continuously variable thyristor drives and numerical controls is forcing machine tool manufacturers who originally confined themselves to mechanical operations to take on production facilities and customer service for electronic equipment. If they are unable to do this for lack of expertise in electronics or lack of sufficient financial backing, they can, of course, buy in the electronic equipment. If they do this, they have to accept a significant reduction in the proportion of the added value that they themselves contribute to every machine tool they produce. The decision whether to set up an electronics division, is therefore closely connected with an appraisal of the future technical trend in the machine tool market. If this development is not recognised in good time, the manufacturer is probably forced into buying his control equipment from one of the large firms in the field of electronics.

In order to maintain his profit level in spite of creating a smaller added value, the manufacturer would have to increase his sales by a considerable amount. This might not be possible in the short term in the home market, and he would therefore have to build up an effective export sales organisation in order to exploit the export market potential.

Market changes bring both opportunities and dangers

Future changes in the market are therefore the focus of interest in the second stage of the appraisal. The market never stands still. Every change brings opportunities and dangers – opportunities only if they are recognised in good time and if the firm is prepared for them; dangers always when the firm is taken by surprise.

The important **market changes** which are the sources of opportunities and dangers for the future position of the firm in its traditional market are:

- Technical changes.
- Changes in the composition of the customers.
- Changes in the sales channels.
- Changes in customer habits.
- Changes in price levels.
- Changes in the competition.
- Changes brought about by government action.

The effects of these on the firm's products and its market must be recognised early and their magnitude and direction worked out. Only then is it possible to plan measures to exploit the opportunities and avoid the dangers. A few examples of economic changes in recent years will show the effect on the future market position of the firms that have been affected.

Technical changes

The energy market has been subject to rapid technical change. Coal, for so long the prime source of energy for European industry, was still being assisted by government support for capital investment in 1952. In Germany household coal was rationed until 1956 and industrial supplies until 1957. Then fuel oil began to be used for domestic heating to a significant extent in 1954. As the competitor of coal it had secured 30 per cent of the domestic heating market in 1962, by 1969 over 50 per cent of the total energy demand was being supplied by oil. Coal, which fifteen years ago was a desirable fuel in short supply, is now fighting a desperate defensive action. However, eighteen years after its successful penetration of the energy market, oil now has a new competitor in natural gas, which will have the dominating effect on the character of this market in the 1970s. By 1975 about one-third of all dwellings supplied with gas will use it for heating. From 1965 to 1975 its use for domestic heating will increase by seven times. Nevertheless, natural gas is already threatened by competition from cheap atomic energy, which experts expect will have driven natural gas out of many important markets within fifteen years.

This turbulent development of the energy market has affected many areas of the economy. Not only mining itself has been strongly affected, but manufacturers of mining machinery, boilers and burners were forced to adapt their production programmes to the new market situation. For many firms, it was a matter of life and death to find new products. Many foundries that had specialised in the manufacture of coal stoves went into liquidation in 1966 when the demand fell off rapidly. But the changes could have been foreseen for a long time. In the European coal-mining districts, the economic and political effects of the evolution of the energy market became matters of public concern and led to an extensive measure of state support.

Many other technical changes, which are equally dangerous for firms affected by them, take place without exciting the concern of the public or the government. A large manufacturer making building and insulating materials out of cork had such an experience. The use of cork in the construction industry and in industry generally was replaced by manmade foams, such as polystyrol and polyurethane. New competitors had penetrated the market by skilful promotion methods. In spite of favourable economic conditions in the building market, the firm's turnover dropped substantially until it was taken over in 1969 and lost its independence. Yet, experts had recognised many years previously that the new manmade materials would rapidly penetrate the traditional markets for cork.

Solex Company, which supplies the European motor industry with carburettors is another firm that will have to adapt itself in good time to technical change. It will have to consider very seriously whether and over what timespan carburettors will be superseded by electronic fuel injection such as has already been developed by Volkswagen, Bosch and Bendix. It will have to be prepared to develop similar injection systems and put them on the market, otherwise it risks becoming another victim of technical change.

Consumer goods can be similarly threatened by technical change. About fifteen years ago, gas refrigerators which worked by absorbtion were superseded by electrical refrigerators working by compression, because they had a higher performance at lower energy costs. Gas ones could be made economically by small manufacturers, but the new electrical refrigerators needed an automated production line, and the majority of the manufacturers of refrigerators could not sustain themselves under the new rules of the game. Those that had not recog-

Critical changes in the composition of the customers

nised the situation in good time and had not adapted to the change by altering their production programmes went into liquidation, including some well-known names.

Critical changes in the composition of the customers

Changes in the composition of the customers can have a serious effect on sales and on the required characteristics of the product. Structural changes of this kind have been experienced in the mining and textile industries, in tanneries and in agriculture in the last ten years. They are often characterised by insufficient willingness to invest new capital, a price war to which mainly small and medium firms fall victim, and a trend towards a small number of large firms. For the manufacturer of machines and equipment, it is not only the fall-off in willingness to invest that can be dangerous, but also the changes in the product requirements that follow from the concentration of the market. Larger customers tend to demand larger machine units with higher capacity and a higher degree of automation. And direct selling takes precedence over sales through distributors. A firm that has specialised in the production of the smaller types of machine sold through wholesalers will have to adapt to such changes in good time. A manufacturer of mining machinery will have to consider what will be the effect on the demand for his machines of the decline in coal consumption and in the number of productive pits. On the one hand, the decline in coal production will lead to a decline in investment for expansion, but, on the other hand, the concentration of coal production in a smaller number of more efficient pits will favour investment for cost-improvement programmes and accelerate the trend towards larger units of mining machinery.

A manufacturer of pesticides or tractors will have to consider the structural changes in agriculture brought about by the decline of small farms and the greater proportion of large agricultural concerns. He will have to work out the effect on the demand for his products, on their technical characteristics and on his sales channels, and how he can respond to such changes.

Changes in sales channels

The situation in the retail grocery trade has been marked in the past ten years by a sharp increase in the market share of supermarkets, chain stores and discount stores. Between 1960 and 1970 these new sales channels took 60 per cent of the trade in baby foods, previously the domain of chemists.

The handling of these new sales channels demands not only a different organisation of the sales force, but also a different sales policy in respect of trade discounts and price fixing. Thus the handling of the non-specialist trade may best be done by a separate organisation using a separate brandname. The firm that was the undisputed market leader in the German baby food market until 1961 decided to stay loyal to the specialist outlets. It thereby abandoned the market reached through the grocery trade to new competitors. One can understand why its market share shrank with the growing importance of new sales channels and why new competitors were able to penetrate the market.

The Dutch quality chocolate manufacturer van Houten was affected by the structural shift in the grocery trade. The firm did not alter its sales policy quickly enough. Its sales representatives called assiduously on the 'corner shops', while the supermarkets and chain stores were neglected. The result was that the firm's market share shrank and declining revenue was confronted by high costs.

Other consumer goods also display a shift in the sales channels. Over 50 per cent of all bicycles are now sold by discount stores and departmental stores, whereas ten years ago the specialist cycle trade dominated the market.

The transition from exclusive selling through the specialist trade to sales through grocery shops and discount stores demands not only a more effective sales organisation, but also greater advertising and sales promotion effort and the abandonment of fixed prices. The decline of fixed prices and exclusive sales outlets can force a change in sales policy. The market opportunities for a manufacturer of toiletries sold principally through specialist outlets may be seriously affected by such changes.

Shifts in sales channels are also found in capital goods. Until 1960 cement and aggregate for the production of concrete were sold exclusively to construction firms. In 1970 50 per cent of the aggregate and cement used for making concrete for building sites on the European continent was sold to a small group of ready-mixed concrete firms who process the material themselves and sell it as concrete to building firms. Suppliers of aggregate who did not adjust to the change and did not themselves participate in the ready-mixed concrete industry soon found themselves cut off from their traditional markets.

Changes in consumer habits

In a very few years following 1952 the motor-cycle industry was the victim of a sudden change in the attitude of German drivers. The motor-cycle, hitherto the means of transport preferred by the working and middle classes, had to give way to the mini-car, and many manufacturers lost their markets. The bicycle manufacturers had a similar experience, although they have been enjoying a recovery since 1967, the bicycle as leisure-equipment and the folding bicycle for car drivers short of exercise having opened up new sales opportunities for them.

The demand for a German coffee-substitute called Kathreiner had been falling annually by about 8 per cent since 1952 partly in consequence of the reduction in the tax on coffee. The private brand made by the same firm lost three-quarters of its sales in ten years. This was the firm's principal product, but they took note of the change in consumer habits and the demand for higher living standards, and introduced in good time a new programme of branded goods: a soluble malt-coffee called Caro and quality specialities, such as mayonnaise, mustard, tomato ketchup, etc, under the brand name Thomy's. Through these prompt changes in its product policies the firm was able to assure its continued existence.

Changes in price levels: the effect of collapsing prices

The leisure market offers new possibilities for a number of industries: caravans, sports goods, hotels, sailing boats, etc, are a growing market. Increased leisure time and the shortage of manual workers led to the rapid growth of 'do-it-yourself': tools, building materials and fittings are being sold not only through the traditional trade outlets, but through specialist handicrafts shops and department stores to the private consumer. Several firms have skilfully helped to create and exploit a large market for electric drills as a result of this trend.

The traditional outlets for building materials and tools have hardly begun to recognise the possibilities. The typical builders' yard shuts at 5 p.m. on weekdays and all day Saturdays, so office workers cannot buy from them. Other traders have exploited the opening. Specialist DIY shops and sections of department stores and discount stores are devoted to the leisure worker and hobbyist, a market which is expected to reach £2 billion in the EEC countries by 1975.

Changes in price levels: the effect of collapsing prices

The future position of the firm in its market can be damaged considerably by changes in price levels.

Some prices have collapsed in an apparently unpredictable way. But in many market areas this is a typical phenomenon that accompanies the entry of a product into the phase of market saturation, and for the trained market observer it is not unexpected. In 1963 certain types of integrated circuit (semi-conductors) cost well over £10 each. Two years later they were offered for £4 and in 1967 for £1. At the end of 1970 the market collapsed because of over-capacity, and severe competition brought the price down to £0·25 each. Even large firms such as Fairchild, Motorola, Philips and Siemens were affected by this collapse of prices.

Electric refrigerators had a similar evolution. In the twenty years from 1950 to 1970 the retail selling price of a standard domestic refrigerator fell from over £100 to around £30. The refrigerators were all of similar quality; indeed, after 1960, they were technically improved models. The fall in prices was the consequence of going over from small batch to mass production and was assisted by serious over-capacity of the manufacturers and the importation of Italian refrigerators. The result was that many firms had to go out of the market altogether, and even large firms, such as Bosch, Brown-Boveri, Philips, Westinghouse, General Electric, Siemens, AEG and Linde, either closed down their refrigerator production or imported refrigerators from Italy which they sold under their own brand names.

The Westphalian cement industry was threatened by a disastrous collapse in prices. From 1966 to 1970 the price per ton of cement fell from £7 to £3, which was far below the production cost. This was caused by the construction of heavy excess capacity in consequence of a cost-improvement programme. In

1962 a modern kiln had an output of 200 tons per day: a few years later 2000-ton kilns were being built. These super-kilns had significantly lower production costs, so that the cement firms found themselves forced to construct them. At the same time the price agreement (cartel) which had existed for a long time collapsed because of a government ban. The consequence was a collapse of prices, to which many medium-sized firms fell victim, and which also had a significant effect on the balance sheets of the large firms in the industry.

A disastrous price collapse was also to be expected in another industry with 'forced rationalisation investment'. Since 1965 the economically superior container-ship is being built in every important shipyard. The consequent excess of shipping space soon resulted in a serious collapse of freight rates. The critical observer of the shipping and ship-building industry could only be surprised by the fact that management of these industries did not anticipate this predictable price-deterioration early enough to counteract it.

Changes in the competition

The liberalisation of external trade can lead to a sudden shift in the competition. Because of the removal of customs duties within the Common Market, Italian manufacturers of washing-machines and similar household equipment were able to move into a dominating position in the French and German markets in the course of a very few years. They succeeded not only in driving many medium-sized German firms out of the market, but even forcing large firms to make new dispositions. They either closed down their washing-machine lines (e.g. Bosch, Siemens and Constructor) or bought an interest in the competition, such as AEG in Zanussi or Philips NV in Ignis, in order to secure a share in the Italians' business. Italian manufacturers of domestic air-conditioners are now penetrating the markets of their Common Market partners equally vigorously. German and English manufacturers of air-conditioners may have little chance of survival in the face of Delchi and Riello which are cheap and of technically outstanding design. Even the American imports, which once dominated the European markets, are being quickly forced to the wall.

A model example of rapid change in the competitive situation in consequence of liberalisation is the rise of Japanese manufacturers of mosaic tiles. Up to 1960 this market, worth £6 million, was dominated by five German firms which had formed a cartel. The situation was characterised by excessive trade discounts and tightly controlled sales channels: only certain wholesalers were supplied. The Japanese recognised the gap in the market. By skilfully avoiding the traditional wholesalers and by offering favourable prices, they succeeded in capturing the market within a very few years. In 1968 they had more than 70 per cent of it.

The effects of Britain's entry into the Common Market ought to be checked within the framework of company planning in the industries concerned, in order to anticipate adverse effects in good time.

Not only imports, but also powerful home competitors can make lasting changes in the market data. An example is the appearance of the American firm of

Proctor & Gamble in the German washing powder business, which until then had been the domain of Henkel, Palmolive and Sunlight.

Changes brought about by government action

Government actions in the political and economic fields can have a significant influence on the market position of a firm, and their significance and effects must be recognised in good time.

Target projections for the national economy – at least in Western Germany and most western countries – are political declarations of intent, quantified in terms of economic objectives. From the standpoint of company planning they are only very general statements about objectives in respect of full employment, price stability, rate of growth of the GNP and stability of external balance of payments. They do not say what concrete economic measures would lead to the achievement of these goals. They are not detailed plans, and consequently, they form no usable basis for company planning.

Nor have the economic forecasts of the ministries of economics established as yet their suitability for use as orientations for the short-term dispositions of companies. In 1968 a growth in the West German GNP of $4\frac{1}{2}$ per cent was forecast for 1969; in fact it was 9 per cent. At the beginning of 1970 the Minister of Economic Affairs and his so-called experts were expecting a decline in economic activity before the middle of the year; in fact it increased still further up to the end of the year.

Concrete government economic plans are another matter: for example, the intention to build container terminals for the German railways, the extension of trunk data transmission services by the Post Office, the five year plans for road construction and transport, etc. These have concrete, measureable effects on the sales opportunities of the firm.

New laws and regulations can have a sharp effect on sales. Changes in the regulations about driving licences for two-wheeled vehicles in the 1950s had a very unfavourable effect on the sales of motor-cycles, but helped the demand for mopeds.

In the 1970s, increased official activity is to be expected in the area of traffic safety, air and water pollution, consumer protection and public health.

In the USA the ban on cyclamates as food additives caused a sharp drop in sales of diet foods. The sales of European manufacturers of cyclamate sweeteners have also suffered from official interference and their future sales opportunities have been damaged.

The cigarette industry with its multi-billion sales is threatened by the possibility of strict limitations on advertising. The possibility of future restrictions on the actual sale of cigarettes cannot be completely ruled out. Company planning in this industry must take account of these potential dangers. It is not for nothing that well-known cigarette firms are seeking a 'second string' by diversifying into other branches of industry.

The small business has special opportunities in a changing market

In appraising the future competitive situation, the capability of the competition and of the firm itself must be carefully checked. But what has been said above must not be taken to mean that changes in the market always threaten small firms and exclude them from competing successfully. On the contrary, experience shows that small- and medium-sized firms may well be able to maintain their position, even in markets characterised by severe competition from the large firms. It is often a matter of finding a niche in the market or a partial market and handling it in an intensive and well-directed manner, so as to make the most of the advantages of a small firm, such as its greater flexibility, and ability to react quickly in comparison with its large competitors.

The firm of Miele is an instructive example. In the last ten years the market for washing-machines and dishwashers has developed into a typical mass market, characterised by continually falling prices and severe competition. Many firms that had previously been active in this area were driven out. Even large firms, such as Siemens, AEG, Bosch and Brown-Boveri, were compelled either to close down their production lines or to take machines supplied by Italian manufacturers.

The firm of Miele consciously chose a segment of this market, namely, the high-quality line. Its products are sold at fixed prices which are usually 10 per cent to 20 per cent higher than those of comparable competing models. In spite of this, Miele machines sell well to quality-conscious consumers who are ready to pay a higher price for these machines. This skilful marketing policy is accompanied by intensive advertising to support the quality image of the firm.

A family tractor business called Fendt maintained its lead in its chosen market against such competition as John Deere, International Harvester and Massey-Ferguson. The recipe for its success was limitation of its programme to small and medium tractors and self-driven agricultural implements, and concentration of sales through the agricultural cooperatives which are particularly effective in this market.

Checklist 2 The company appraisal

Part 1 The current situation

The market

1 In which markets do our products have a part to play?
2 How big is the total market?

— Home, Common Market, Europe, overseas.

3 What is the share of the separate market segments?
— By the nature, age, size, etc, of the user.
— By the nature of the demand (first purchase, replacement purchase).
— By sales channels.

4 What important factors influence the customers' decision to select this brand of product?

— Technical properties, performance, capacity.
— Shape, colour, styling.
— Sales density, customer service.
— Price, discount, trading terms.
— Manufacturer's reputation (image).

The firm

1 What is the firm's share of the market now?

— In total – home – Common Market – Europe.
— In the individual market segments.

2 What is the customers' appraisal of our products?

3 How good is our performance, taking account of brand selection criteria and future requirements?

4 Where are the strengths and weaknesses of our firm in respect of manpower, finance, products, product development, production technology, sales?

The competitors

1 What are their market shares?

— Home – Common Market – Europe.
— In the individual market segments.

2 What is the customers' appraisal of their products?

3 What are the strengths and weaknesses of the most important competitors in respect of finance, products, product development, production technology, sales?

Checklist 2 The company appraisal

Part 2 Future developments

The market

1 How will the requirements and habits of the customers change in the future?

— Technical requirements on the product.
— Sales channels.
— Customer service.

2 How will the demand develop?

— Home – Common Market – Europe – Overseas.
— By the nature, age, size, etc, of the consumers.
— By the nature of the demand (first or subsequent purchase).

3 How will prices and margins develop?

4 How will the composition of the customers change in the future?

5 Will new suppliers enter the market?

The firm and its future opportunities

1 What market shares can we expect in the future if we continue on our present course?

2 What future market share can we expect if:

— The products are modernised?
— The product range is extended?
— The sales effort is intensified?

3 What changes in sales strategy are possible, in order to increase turnover?

— New sales channels.
— Attacking certain market segments more strongly.
— Better direction of the sales force.

4 What resources will be needed for such changes, in respect of manpower, development, capital?

5 Will the financial resources be sufficient?

6 Will specialists be needed? Of what level? How many?

7 What organisation changes will be needed in the firm or in the sales division?

4

Formulating the company objectives

In setting the company objectives we are trying to answer the **question**:

Where should the firm stand in five or seven years' time?

It must be clearly recognised from the outset that deciding on company objectives is not a purely rational process, and that the decision is strongly influenced by irrational factors.

An important objective, frequently mentioned at annual meetings, is to increase the turnover and profit of the firm. In 1962 Mr Harold Geneen, President of ITT, set his colleagues in management the task of doubling turnover and profit within five years. The objective was reached.

Rapid growth can bring important **advantages** to the firm:

- Through higher turnover, unit costs of production, purchases, sales and advertising can be reduced, and the firm is thereby better able to withstand competition.
- The firm becomes a dynamic organisation that attracts good managers: new jobs and promotion opportunities can be offered to younger personnel, and the top executive positions do not ossify, as can be the case in stagnating firms.
- Because the financial world is oriented towards growth, it is easier to gain access to the capital market and to raise capital on favourable terms.

But it must not be overlooked that excessively **rapid growth** also brings **dangers** for the firm:

- The organisation can go out of control, with the result that costs rise rapidly and the quality of the products or of the customer service falls off.
- Cash problems can arise, especially if unexpected difficulties occur during a phase of rapid growth; for example, depressed economic conditions, excessively strong competition or a drop in the price level.

One must, however, accept in practice that growth of turnover and profits will be in the forefront of considerations about company objectives. The fetish of growth which prevails in present-day political economy will look after this.

Growth objectives should be defined as concretely as possible, for example:

- Growth of turnover in line with growth in the GNP.
- A specified rate of growth for the firm, such as doubling turnover and profits in five years.
- A rate of growth higher by a specified percentage than the rate of growth in the industry to which the firm belongs.

In addition to or instead of growth there are **other objectives** that may make sense for the firm or its owners; for example:

- Improvement in the return on turnover or on capital. This can often be achieved by rationalisation, reorganisation, product standardisation or changes in sales methods, rather than by increasing turnover.
- Securing the independent existence of the firm, if it is threatened by excessive competition or a crisis in its industry. This objective often demands changes in the organisation or financial structure of the firm in addition to changes in the product list or the sales channels.
- Creating the conditions for a smooth transfer of the firm to the owner's children. A concrete objective for this purpose might be the creation of two independent divisions of the firm ready to be handed over to two sons of the proprietor, so that each can be his own master, which might be achieved by building up a second string (diversification) or by creating two separate operating divisions of the firm with independent production and sales facilities.
- Changing the structure of the organisation of the firm, in order to separate ownership and management at a later stage. The author's experience has shown that this objective is particularly important for owners who have no suitable successors to put into the firm. Such a distinction secures the future income of members of the family and heirs, and is in practice a very important condition for a possible future sale of the firm on favourable terms. On grounds of cost such a change in the management structure will often be impossible without an improvement in profits.
- Securing the firm's independence of economic swings and of structural changes in its traditional market. This is an objective that should be seriously considered even if the firm is showing satisfactory returns. It involves a basic business decision about achieving security by spreading the risk.

Setting objectives is a task for the directors

The objectives selected by a company will always be conditioned by its situation and the personal situation of its owner, his mode of life and willingness to go in and take risks. In private firms the dominating questions should be those of security, of regulating the owner's income and the future management of the firm after the retirement of the owner, whereas companies with wide participation in their ownership should give first consideration to questions of returns and growth.

Both kinds of firm can use company planning to good effect, in order to ensure that the consciously selected objectives are in fact achieved. But only the owner or the directors who carry full responsibility for the firm at board level can declare the company objectives and commit the company to them.

This task cannot under any circumstances be left to the staff personnel of the planning section or to outside consultants. Such personnel can make significant contributions to the setting up of alternative objectives and alternative plans for reaching them, and can work out their consequences. These are important aids to the owner or directors in making their decision.

Experience shows that the apparently simple task of setting company objectives presupposes a series of deep-lying personal decisions – all the more so, because the firm is going to be committed to these objectives in writing. It is the moment of truth for those responsible.

Especially for the private entrepreneur, the question that is mercilessly posed is that of his motives and objectives and of his commitment to the firm. He should not make his decision lightly or under pressure of time. It is better first to make a rough draft of company objectives, and then to think about them and discuss them with friends and relations for a considerable time, before accepting a specific objective with full conviction and determination, and committing oneself to it in writing. Later changes in the objectives will mean that the operating plans have to be reworked; this is both expensive and time-wasting.

Brief formulations carry conviction

When formulating company objectives, their psychological effect should be considered. This is particularly important in large firms where a large number of managers are actively concerned in the realisation of the objectives. It is therefore necessary to express company objectives in clear, simple and convincing language.

In his inauguration speech President J. F. Kennedy said:
'It is our intention during this decade to put a man on the moon and to bring him safely back.'

'The moon was an impressive and pregnant objective. Everybody knows what the moon is, everybody knows what 1970 is. That was the kernel of the Apollo programme.' This was how Wernher von Braun expressed it in a talk after the first successful moon-landing.

This inspiring formulation of the task was effective. Congress enthusiastically authorised the means for the realisation of the space flight plan, which cost $35 000 million between 1959 and 1969.

If Kennedy had said, 'We wish to learn how to move about the cosmos,' Congress would probably have debated the necessary measures and the authorisation of the means for many years without coming to a clear decision.

Whether Kennedy's moon objective was inherently sound and more sensible than the abolition of social distress, or the development of cures for cancer or influenza – objectives which might have been achieved in the same period for £15 000 million – is a question that must remain unanswered. It is customary for objectives to be chosen on irrational grounds. The American architect Wilbur H. Burnham coined the phrase: 'Don't make little plans – they don't set men's blood coursing.' In business, too, the formulation of company objectives needs a shot of demagogy – but not too much.

General principles must be supported by concrete objectives

A chemical firm in Ludwigshafen set itself the concrete objective of increasing the turnover from £25 million in 1970 to £50 million in 1975, while investing £10 million of new capital, but this was to be achieved without departing from the principle of being a family firm and without significantly extending its product range.

If growth and return on capital are strongly emphasised as yardsticks of success and of future objectives, the importance of remaining within the firm's traditional branch of industry is diminished. In these circumstances the owner or directors must consider more carefully what they regard as the mission or *raison d'être* of their firm. The following definition of their mission given by the giant American detergent firm of Proctor & Gamble is instructive:

We are first of all a firm that is master of the modern marketing techniques. We wish to remain so. Our planning must therefore take account of every possibility for expansion in which our skill in marketing would be decisive of success or failure.

Instead of concrete formulae, like doubling turnover and profit in five years, general business principles are sometimes set up as objectives; for example:

- A long-term growth in returns that is as large as possible.
- A leading position in the industry, in respect of technical product development, price leadership, highly qualified personnel, higher than average wage and salary rates, etc.
- A commitment to active participation in community and national tasks, and to social responsibility.

American firms in particular have developed an inclination towards such declarations of faith in the last twenty years.

But it turns out that, for example, the general principle of price or quality leadership may come into conflict in day-to-day practice with the pressures of market segmentation. Is it reasonable that a firm should refuse to supply a cheap unbranded washing powder for discount stores or a simple electric motor for cheap lawnmowers in the original equipment market, simply because it has proclaimed that its company objective is to hold the position of price-leader or only to deliver highest quality goods?

Declarations of this kind cannot be used as a basis for company planning if they are not accompanied by concrete objectives with reference to turnover and returns.

This does not mean that the business has to be conducted without regard for political or social needs. But general principles unsupported by concrete objectives are at best only a guideline for the management. They may make it easier to decide between different alternatives. They are usually used in practice for justifying decisions of the management after the event.

Sceptics are of the opinion that general business principles have some value for public relations, but beyond that are as binding in practice as party political platforms before an election.

Again, this does not mean that turnover and returns are the only possible concrete objectives. The checklist on page 33 shows that there are many areas of the firm where it is possible to specify objectives in measurable quantitative terms, and thereby to exercise effective control by comparison of planned and actual figures.

Company objectives must not only be expressed clearly, but must also be realistic. The feasibility of the objectives must be checked and confirmed by detailed implementation plans. If they show that the implementation is impossible, or involves unacceptable risks and sacrifices, the objectives must be revised.

The H-bomb syndrome

A source of dangerous mistakes in the setting of company objectives is the 'H-bomb syndrome'. Because he believed that a nation could only become a great power by possessing hydrogen bombs and the means to deliver them, President de Gaulle strove to reach this objective without regard to its cost, its economic effects or its limited strategic value. The result was that the country had to go without investment that was urgently needed for the infrastructure and modernisation of the economy. Social tensions followed and the President had to resign.

Companies are also affected by this syndrome. Many European and American firms in the electronics industry strove to develop their own computers without regard to the cost and the competition because 'the future belongs to the computer'. In spite of long years of effort and high development costs, the computer divisions of many important electronics firms such as AEG, Siemens, RCA, Bull, Westinghouse, Philips, General Electric and others lost enormous sums of money and seriously hampered attempts to develop other potentially profitable product lines. Many of these firms finally closed down or sold out their computer division during recent years.

Another example is the attempt made by many engineering firms to develop atomic power stations. Many firms, including large ones such as Babcock and Wilcox have had to give up this objective and write off substantial development costs.

British readers may like to consider whether the 'H-bomb syndrome' played a part in the Rolls-Royce affair, or was at the root of the decision to build the tremendously costly and unprofitable Concorde supersonic airliner.

Experience shows that, when company objectives are being set, the real capabilities and limitations of the firm and the risks that it can carry must never be forgotten. The owner or directors should ask themselves three questions before they finally decide on their objectives:

- What benefit would be brought by the achievement of the objective?
- What costs would be incurred through failure?
- What are the chances of success?

The objectives, the plan and the modification of the objectives are linked by a feedback loop

Setting company objectives is not a once for all action, detached from the other stages of company planning. There is a feedback loop which links setting objectives through confirmation of their feasibility by detailed planning to revision of turnover targets. The effectiveness of this loop is the only solid basis for working towards future objectives of the firm.

Checklist 3 Quantitative planning objectives

Turnover
— Increase in total turnover
— Increase in turnover in particular market segments

Returns
— Increase in profit before tax
— Increase in contribution to overheads
— Improvement in return on capital
— Increase in profit after tax
— Improvement in return on turnover

Finance
— Reduction in debtors as percentage of turnover
— Reduction in the period of outstanding claims
— Reduction in short-term obligations
— Improvement in the ratio of internal to external capital

Production
— Increase in contribution per employee
— Reduction of waste as a percentage of production
— Reduction in the ratio of customer complaints to sales
— Reduction in the ratio of warranty work to sales
— Reduction of late deliveries

Stock control
— Reduction in the value of stocks (finished goods, raw materials, work in progress) in relation to sales

Manpower
— Improvement in the rate of turnover
— Achievement of a specified number of employees

Advertising
— Improvement in the degree of knowledge of the firm by the relevant consumer groups

Sales
— Distribution density
— Number of prospects called upon
— Number of new customers
— Sales costs as a percentage of turnover
— Cost of the sales force as percentage of turnover
— Number of customer inquiries
— Number of offers sent out
— Ratio of offers to orders

5

Market planning

The company appraisal was concerned with the position of the firm in its market and with its prospects of maintaining or enhancing its market position in the future. Market planning is concerned with the **questions**:

- What steps will have to be taken if the company is to reach its objectives within its traditional market?
- Will the company have to enter new markets?

Market planning can be divided into **three stages**:

1 Working out the market strategies which are in principle relevant to the company's objectives.
2 Choosing the market strategies which are most suitable, taking into account risks, cashflow and returns.
3 Planning the short-term and long-term measures needed to implement these strategies.

The market conditions go a long way towards determining the possible ways in which a company can reach its objectives. The success of measures taken to realise the objectives depends to a very great degree on whether market opportunities are skilfully exploited and whether the risks inherent in the development of the market are correctly appraised. That is why market planning occupies a central position in company planning.

Working out the market strategies is a sequential process

When planning market strategies, it makes sense to investigate and exploit the more familiar possibilities first, and only to consider more distant areas

Rationalisation

of activity if the company's objectives cannot be achieved within its own markets.

Psychologically, it is easy to fall for the proverb that 'the grass is always greener on the other side of the fence'. Markets other than one's own always sound more attractive, because one is confronted daily with all the problems of one's own operations, whereas one tends to hear more about the attractions and less about the difficulties of other people's markets.

The author's experience with many companies shows that the following sequence of activities forms the most effective way of reaching company objectives:

1 Rationalisation of sales, production and administration.
2 Intensification of sales, and market segmentation.
3 Increasing sales to foreign markets.
4 Extending the range of products produced.
5 Developing better products.
6 Diversification.

Rationalisation

Rationalisation of current activities often leads not only to increased turnover, but also to reduced costs, so that there is a double benefit to the company's results. Profit targets can often be met partially or wholly by this means alone. Experience indicates a very favourable relation between the results of rationalisation and the cost in time and money. In other words, rationalisation is often the quickest way of bringing about significant improvements in turnover and profit with the least expense and risk. This book is not the place for a thorough treatment of the subject and methods of rationalisation. What follows is a brief note on those areas where, in the author's experience, rationalisation has shown the biggest gains.

Rationalisation of sales offers the possibility of improved turnover and profit in consumer goods and especially in the capital goods industries. This includes planning the effort of the sales force for the most effective impact on existing customers and new prospects, classifying products and orders by the A-B-C system, and withdrawing loss-making products from the lists. A well-directed programme of salesmen's calls, based on a carefully built up index of prospects with good route planning and a correspondingly well-thought-out reporting system, is worth special attention. It is always worth checking warehousing and dispatch for possible savings and improvements.

Cost reduction through improved flow of materials and production methods has been the main concern of rationalisation through work study and method study for half a century.

Value analysis is an important means of reducing the cost of a product without impairing its usefulness to the consumer. The cost savings from value analysis can be used either to increase turnover by lowering prices or to improve profitability by improving margins.

Substantial savings in fixed costs and in labour costs can often be made by pruning the administration and in particular by getting rid of supporting services such as vehicle repair shops, carpenters' shops and construction units, which have grown up like weeds in the last twenty years. In the current state of some labour markets this may be the only available source of additional labour for lucrative and expanding parts of the business.

It is important to emphasise that, when strategies are being selected, such conventional methods of rationalisation as are indicated in checklist 4 should be checked for their potential contribution to company objectives, before spending time and money on planning and implementing other measures.

Checklist 4 Rationalisation methods

Production
— Materials flow in production
— Value analysis of the products
— Method improvements
— Larger batch sizes
— Buying parts in, instead of manufacturing them

Distribution
— Too many, or too few, warehouses
— Materials flow in the warehouses
— Methods of dispatch (rail, carrier, own transport)
— Changing the routing of products from the factory to the customer

Sales
— Changing the sales channels (wholesalers, agents, representatives)
— More carefully directed activities of the sales force
— Are all prospects known?
— Are they classified according to importance?
— Are the sales journeys planned in relation to the importance of the prospects?
— Rejection of unprofitable orders, order quantities and products
— Extending the product-line

Intensification of sales

It is often the case that the company objective of increased growth in turnover can be reached through better exploitation of the existing market potential by intensifying the sales effort.

This is how a furniture manufacturer (Richter in Rüdesheim), one of the largest direct suppliers of upholstered furniture, came to the objective of moving away gradually from mailorder and greatly extending its network of retail outlets. From 1966 to 1969 the turnover doubled, from £2 million to £4 million, but the proportion of mailorder business fell. If further expansion was to be achieved, the retail outlets would have to be increased, because the customers were demanding higher value goods and more individual attention. To create the conditions for further growth, the firm was compelled to change and intensify its sales methods. The objective became: change of sales methods from mailorder to the firm's own shops. The action programme for 1970 was to open nine new shops in addition to the existing chain of twenty-six shops.

The intensification of sales effort can only be planned successfully on the basis of a systematic selling policy, or in other words *marketing*. The planning must start from the market, i.e. the customers with their needs and desires, the sales channels and the competition. A marketing plan can only be implemented in practice if the market conditions are known in advance. Market research is usually necessary. Based on its findings, a **marketing study** then investigates the questions:

- Whether an increase in the market share and in turnover by X per cent is feasible?
- What measures are needed to reach the target?

Checklists 5 and 6 show the most important questions that have to be investigated in market research and market planning.

The capital goods industries are especially weak in their approach to the market: they often attack it either irrationally or half-heartedly. They are still a long way from using systematic study of the market as an everyday marketing tool in the way it is used, for example, in the branded goods industries.

Checklist 5 Market research

1. Who are the potential customers for my products? How are they made up:
   — Kind (sex, age, size, industry, etc)?
   — Number, structure?
   — Geographical location?

2. For what purposes is the product used?

3. What criteria are used by the trade and the consumer in selecting the preferred brand or manufacturer?

4. What demands are made by the customer in respect of:
   — Properties (performance, size, shape)?
   — Sales, technical advice, customer service?
   — Lead times?
   — Methods of financing?

5. How will these demands change in the future?

6. What share of the demand goes through the different sales channels? What is the future trend?

7. What is the customers' appraisal of the competitors and their products?

8. What sources of information are used by the customer to inform himself about what is being offered?

9. What shares of the market are held by the most important competitors?

10. What kind of sales organisation do the competitors use?

11. Are the customers currently satisfied with the competitors' products, sales and customer service? What are the possible sources of dissatisfaction?

12. Are there still unsolved problems with the products or the customer service? How strongly are they influencing the selection of brand of manufacture?

13. To what extent are the trade and the consumers willing to stock or use a new make of product? What conditions must be satisfied for them to do so? (Price, discounts, quality, customer service.)

Checklist 6 Market planning

1. How must sales be organised to reach the most interesting segments of the market at an acceptable cost?

    — What sales channels can be used?
    — What trade margins have to be allowed?
    — What kind of a sales force is needed to call on customers and the trade (number, specialist qualifications, training)

2. What has to be done in the area of sales promotion and advertising?

    — Advertising: kind, quantity, media
    — Sales aids, brochures, display materials, self-service racks, exhibitions
    — Training of retailers and sales force
    — Technical advice to trade and customer on applications of the product

3. What market shares can be expected from the different sales strategies?

    — What are the expected ratios of turnover and costs?

4. How should distribution be organised?

    — What time interval between order and delivery does the market demand?
    — How many warehouses for products and spare parts are required?
    — Where can products and parts be stored? By the retailers? In the firm's own warehouses?
    — How should dispatch be organised?

5. What level of performance is expected of customer service and spare part service? How can it be achieved?

    — Through the firm's own branches? Through the trade? From the factory?
    — What personnel are needed and what costs will be incurred?

6. What are the possible price policies?

    — Fixed prices, list prices, free prices?
    — What is the price structure for customer service and spares?
    — Reductions, discounts, quantity rebates, credit terms?

Market segmentation

The producer of consumer goods can also be faced with the question of whether the firm is already attacking all segments of the market and exploiting all subsections of it. A producer of toiletry goods who has hitherto been selling only through specialist outlets, has to ask himself seriously whether he can go on doing without the discount stores trade. It is expected that by 1973 20 per cent of the trade in groceries, hardware, tyres, furniture and toiletries will pass through this new form of retailing. A maker of branded goods has to decide how he can participate in the growth of these new channels of distribution. It could be equally important for opening up the full potential of the market to decide whether to produce 'private-label' goods for departmental stores, chain stores, mailorder stores and co-operatives. He will have to examine his brand strategy very carefully. For discount stores and other non-specialist outlets he can offer his products either unbranded, under an alternative brand name or under his own brand name. The alternative brand, the unbranded article and the retailer's 'private label' all offer the possibility of supplying those new channels of distribution without provoking resistance from the specialist trade.

These methods of market segmentation through different forms of the product, different packaging and different pricing, form an effective way of attacking several sectors of the markets simultaneously and thereby exploiting more fully the potential of the whole market.

Similar market segmentation strategies are also possible for capital goods. The smaller customers are often more concerned about a lower purchase cost than they are about operating convenience or output performance. A large customer is likely to be more ready to pay for quality and performance in machines. The different factors that influence purchasing behaviour form the starting point for a segmentation of the market, e.g. by adding a 'basic' machine to the range so that orders can be obtained from the smaller prospective users.

Expanding into export markets

Most European firms export their products, but many of them have hitherto treated the EEC market as normal export business and have traded through importers. In this way they lose out on the opportunities and growing importance of the EEC market. Many firms that have a strong position in the home market have a very weak one in the markets of their neighbours in the EEC. In these circumstances a firm should examine carefully the opportunity for increasing turnover through intensified export sales policies. It may be worth building up customer service stations in EEC countries to support the importers, building up one's own distribution network, or constructing local factories either as

c

wholly owned subsidiaries or jointly with foreign partners. The situation in other European export markets and in the USA may be similar, but before setting targets of that kind a firm would be well advised to make sure that it has exhausted the market opportunities in the EEC where the general trading conditions are so much more favourable. At the same time it must be recognised that different EEC countries make different demands on the product and have different kinds of sales channels, to which the firm must accommodate itself. In spite of these difficulties, it is possible to achieve substantial increases in turnover by going over from general export trading through importers to intensive cultivation of a particular export market by the firm itself, as is practised in the home market. In addition, this represents a spreading of the risk, because it is easier for a strong sales organisation in a foreign country to compensate for a drop in home sales.

Extending the range of the production programme

By extending the range of products produced, it may be possible for the firm to satisfy a larger proportion of the customers' needs. The most important effects are: more effective use of the sales force, and reduction of selling costs along with increase in turnover. An extension of the product range could lead, for example, to a manufacturer of agricultural tractors producing combine harvesters and other agricultural equipment, or a manufacturer of road rollers producing other road construction machinery. A well-known toilet-paper firm (Hakle) extended its range to include polishing cloths and similar household goods. Volkswagen have been trying for the past ten years, with variable success, to add upper middle-class vehicles to the beetle in order to obtain a larger share of the total market by satisfying the customers' desire for bigger cars.

Developing better products

The purpose of making significant improvements to the product is to strengthen its competitive position in the market, to increase its market share and to revitalise sales. But there is no point in adopting this strategy unless the firm's products are actually susceptible to significant improvements, which the customer is willing to acknowledge, either by paying a higher price or by switching brands. Technical improvement is an important competitive weapon in many markets, but there are some in which it has virtually no part to play. Medicines sold over the counter are an example. Aspirin has held a dominating position in the market for pain relievers for well over half a century: its chemical composition has not been changed since it was introduced by Bayer in 1899. Washing powders, cigarettes, motor-cars and radio-receivers are other examples of what are probably fully-ripened markets in which further technical developments are unlikely to lead to any significant competitive advantage.

Diversification

We speak of 'diversification' when a firm decides to manufacture products which are either used by existing customers for new applications or which take the firm into completely new markets. Diversification is not a matter of extending the product range, but of fundamentally changing the product range or the market.

In a branch of industry with a low growth rate or strong competition, diversification may be the only way of implementing ambitious company objectives. In the last ten years European firms have become increasingly diversification-conscious, and because it is one of the most important company planning strategies it has been made the subject of a separate chapter.

How to choose between alternative strategies by using the 'gap' method

The second stage of marketing planning consists of checking how the possible strategies mentioned on the preceeding pages will affect sales and profits, and deciding, on the basis of this investigation, which of the strategies should be considered for the realisation of the company objectives.

Before a choice can be made, all the strategies that are in principle feasible must first be investigated. It is often necessary to test several different implementation plans for a single strategy. Thus in order to test the strategy of widening the market, it is necessary to check which export markets should be entered, and in each case whether by using a general distributor, building up the firm's own sales organisation, issuing licences, installing production facilities independently or in some form of association with other firms. The alternatives that show the best profit and returns are provisionally selected and the effects of each of these alternatives, not only on turnover and sales, but also on return on capital and cashflow, are checked.

Evaluating the alternatives from the point of view of profitability and capital requirements often leads to some of them being dismissed immediately, without the necessity of comparing them with other possibilities. It may turn out, for example, that to establish a sales organisation of one's own in a foreign country leads to a considerable increase in turnover, but is unprofitable or needs too much capital. A similar fate can befall the strategy 'product development' on grounds of profitability or of the amount of time or capital that will probably be needed. In such cases the strategy in question has to be given up and is not further discussed. In the example shown here, of a manufacturer of construction machinery, the elimination of the possible strategy 'product development' because it would need too much capital means that the company will have to find the required additional turnover of £0·2 million from elsewhere by diversification – assuming, of course, that the detailed planning shows that diversification is feasible from the point of view of profitability and capital requirements.

The final choice among the pretested strategies can best be made with the help of so-called 'gap-planning'. All the individual strategies of a conventional nature are considered first, and their cumulative effect on turnover and profits is estimated. Only those strategies are taken into account which have already been shown to reach the required level of profitability, and to involve risks and capital requirements that fall within acceptable limits.

Two complete examples of choosing market strategies are shown on the following pages, first for a manufacturer of construction equipment for the building industry and then for a manufacturer of consumer goods, namely, sunglasses. What each intended to do in respect of rationalisation, sales intensification, expanding into export markets, extending the product range and product improvement is shown in tabular form. In both cases diversification is shown to be necessary if the company objectives are to stand, because other measures do not suffice to meet them. Alternatively the company objectives will have to be revised.

The action programmes for the first year show what will have to be done in the companies' customary area of work. Diversification usually takes a longer time to prepare and has to be worked out first in the planning section. It therefore appears in the action programme for the planning section and for top management.

The objectives and methods of market planning do not differ in principle between the manufacturer of capital goods and the manufacture of consumer goods. It will be seen, however, that the producer of consumer goods has to pay much more attention to the possibilities of market segmentation and opening up new sales channels if he is to make a realistic appraisal of the opportunities for growth in his area.

Example 1 A manufacturer of construction equipment
Planning period 1973–1978

Part 1 Alternative market strategies

STRATEGY	DESCRIPTION
1 Do nothing	Growth in turnover follows from natural growth of total demand. No important changes are made in sales or production.
2 Rationalisation	
(a) Production	Cease to manufacture axles and steering gear. Buy them in.
(b) Spares	Close four spare parts sub-depots, leaving one central depot. Reorganise, to deliver orders by rail express (orders received up to 17.00 hours delivered to 90 per cent of all towns in West Germany by 10.00 next day).
(c) Sales	Sales offices will maintain hand stocks of replacement parts. Existing arrangements with six main agents withdrawn. Employ six sales representatives operating from Head Office and from four branch sales offices.
3 Intensification of sales	Hitherto only building firms were called on. In future call on the larger producers of building materials and gravel pits. Take part in two trade fairs. A card index of prospective customers will be set up in A-B-C categories and journey planning will be done. This will lead to more prospective customers being more effectively handled without additional representatives.
4 Expanding into foreign markets	
(a) France	Dispense with the present importer in Paris. Start a new sales company with an associated firm.
(b) Italy	Establish a branch sales office in Milan. Dispense with present Milan agent; agents in Genoa and Rome to be retained, but as 'subagents'.
(c) USA	Establish a subsidiary company, at first for sales and customer service only, but later to have its own assembly plant.
5 Extending the product range	Snow-clearers to be added as attachments; the applications of the existing machine are thereby extended.
6 Product improvement	Develop a torque-converter to replace the present hand-operated gearbox, thus improving performance and comfort.
7 Diversification	Extend the programme into completely new markets (agriculture, transport) or products (hydraulic excavators, fork-lift stackers), or lateral diversification.

Example 1 A manufacturer of construction equipment
Planning period 1973–1978 *(cont.)*
Part 2 Choosing between alternative market strategies

STRATEGY	ESTIMATED INCREASE IN TURNOVER AND PROFIT BY 1978 (£000)	COMMENTS AFFECTING THE CHOICE
1 Do nothing	Turnover + £200 Profit + £10	Natural growth in demand estimated at 30 per cent, but passive attitude would lead to loss of market share to active competitors and shrinking margins, and in the long term would endanger the existence of the firm. Not acceptable as the sole strategy.
2 Rationalisation		
(a) Production	Turnover no change Profit + £10	No disadvantages in respect of market position. Implement at once.
(b) Spares	Turnover no change Profit + £20	No disadvantages in respect of market position. Build up central organisation at once. Until branch sales offices have been established, representatives will hold their own hand stocks.
(c) Sales	Turnover + £150 Profit + £30	To avoid high cost of compensation for dismissed agents, get rid of the worst two in 1973. Two more will retire on grounds of age in 1976 and 1977, and will not be replaced by sales representatives until then. Sales channels to be changed step by step, not all at once.
3 Intensification of sales	Turnover + £150 Profit + £30	Agents who have not yet been dismissed must plan their contacts on the basis of the card index of potential customers. Reporting system to be improved.
4 Expanding into export markets		
(a) France	Turnover + £250 Profit + £20	The importer's contract expires mid 1974. The sales company must be working by then. Return is satisfactory, capital requirement can be met.

Example 1

STRATEGY	ESTIMATED INCREASE IN TURNOVER AND PROFIT BY 1978 (£000)	COMMENTS AFFECTING THE CHOICE
(b) Italy	Turnover + £250 Profit + £10	The contract with the agent in Milan cannot be terminated until 1975. Delay implementation of this strategy until 1975.
(c) USA	Turnover + £100 Profit + £20	No experience with USA. Suitable managers not available. Capital requirement more than can be met from existing resources. Risk too great. Strategy rejected.

5 Extending the product range

	Turnover + £150 Profit + £20	Can only be carried out by buying in, as the quantities are too small to be produced by us. Decision: formulate a programme and introduce by 1974.

6 Product improvement

	Turnover + £150 Profit + £20	Must be done, in order to strengthen our competitive position and maintain it in the long term. Own development work too expensive and not profitable. Look for suitable suppliers. Introduce the new machine in 1974.

* Total planned increases:	Turnover £1·3m	Profit £0·17m
Company growth objective:	Turnover £1·5m	Profit £0·2m
Gap:	Turnover £0·2m	Profit £0·03m.

7 Diversification

	Turnover + £200 Profit + £30	The need for diversification follows from the gap between company objectives (doubling turnover and profit by 1977) and the probable results of the strategies so far thought to be feasible.

Example 1 A manufacturer of construction equipment Planning period 1973–1978 *(cont.)*

Part 3. Action programme for 1973

DEPRTMENT	WORK PROGRAMME
Design	Evaluate axles and steering gear available from home and foreign suppliers. Establish a list of suitable types. Evaluate available attachments for snow clearing. Establish a specification and a list of suitable suppliers. Evaluate and test available torque-converters. Present results by end of 1973.
Purchasing	Obtain offers of axles, steering gear and snow clearers on the basis of information supplied by Design Department.
Customer Service	Reorganise central spare parts store and hand stocks with representatives and agents. Adjust quantities to meet new demands. Reduce or close down subdepots. Prepare customer service for snow clearers.
Sales Management	
(a) Home	Train two new representatives. Dismiss two agents. Set up prospective customer index, grouped on A-B-C principle. Set up journey plans for representatives and agents, reorganise reporting methods. Prepare for participation in two trade fairs.
(b) Export	Build up sales subsidiary in France by early 1974. Train personnel. Take steps to terminate contract with French importer.
Personnel	Recruit two home sales representatives, and staff for French subsidiary. Investigate transfer of personnel in four subdepots to other departments, or give them notice. Check on existing personnel suitable for Milan sales office. Establish training needs (marketing, languages) and make proposals to Sales Management. Recruit transmission specialist for Design Department.
Company Planning	Begin diversification planning, to fill gap in objectives.
MD's office	Choose an external consultant to help with diversification planning.

Example 2 A manufacturer of sunglasses
Planning period 1973–78
Part 1 Alternative market strategies

STRATEGY	DESCRIPTION
1 Do nothing	Growth in turnover follows from natural growth of total demand. No important changes are made in sales or production.
2 Rationalisation	
(a) Production	Install a machine with good performance for manufacturing plastic lenses.
(b) Distribution	Wholesalers to be supplied only in standard dozen packs. No broken packs.
(c) Administration	Customer accounts, delivery documents, invoices and stock control documents to be produced by EDP using a computer service.
3 Intensification of sales	
(a) Shop promotions	Put special sales promoters into selected department stores to promote sale of sunglasses. Store takes a share of turnover.
(b) Fashion programme	Hitherto only a standard line was offered. Introduce high fashion lines at higher prices and sell through special outlets (boutiques, fashion shops).
(c) Private label	Introduce a cheap line for bulk supply to a petrol firm for sale in accessory shops at petrol stations.
4 Expanding into export markets	
(a) France	Dispense with importer. Set up a French sales office.
(b) Sweden	Virtually no sales up to now. Find an effective importer.
5 Extending the product range	Build up a line of ski-glasses and create a brand name. Sell through sports shops and sports departments of stores in Germany and Austria. Create new sales organisation for this purpose.
6 Diversification	Enter new markets, such as protective goggles for industry, optical spectacles, scientific products in plastics, toys, etc.

Example 2 A manufacturer of sunglasses
Planning period 1973–78 *(cont.)*
Part 2. Choosing between alternative market strategies

STRATEGY	ESTIMATED INCREASE IN TURNOVER AND PROFIT BY 1978 (£000)	COMMENTS AFFECTING THE CHOICE
1 Do nothing	Turnover + £50 Profit no change	Increase in leisure time will lead to growth in total demand of about 10 per cent p.a. But cheap lines are being increasingly imported from Italy and Hong Kong. Threat of loss of market. Not acceptable as the sole strategy.
2 Rationalisation		
(a) Production	Turnover no change Profits + £10	No disadvantages with respect to marketing, return on investment satisfactory. Install in 1973.
(b) Distribution	Turnover no change Profit + £10	No disadvantages with respect to marketing, implement in 1973.
(c) Administration	Turnover no change Profit + £10	No disadvantages with respect to marketing, implement in 1973.
3 Intensification of sales		
(a) Shop promotions	Turnover + £120 Profit + £20	Limited programme only, to avoid conflict with wholesalers. Implement in 1973.
(b) Fashion programme	Turnover + £120 Profit + £30	This is new territory for the firm, which was not previously fashion-oriented. Hence, a high risk strategy. Restrict at first to a test market. Prepare a product range and test market, and supply from 1974.

Example 2

STRATEGY	ESTIMATED INCREASE IN TURNOVER AND PROFIT BY 1978 (£000)	COMMENTS AFFECTING THE CHOICE
(c) Private label	Turnover + £80 Profit + £10	No disadvantages with respect to marketing. Will help to belance load on production. Implement 1973.

4 Expanding into export markets

(a) France	Turnover + £150 Profit + £10	Market opportunities too limited and selling costs too high. Not to be carried out.
(b) Sweden	Turnover + £80 Profit + £10	No disadvantages, no serious risk. Implement 1973.

5 Extending the product range, ski-glasses

	Turnover + £200 Profit + £30	Rapid increase in ski-ing will lead to growth in demand. Well established competitors will make market penetration difficult. Two years' preparation needed for styling, product development, etc. Prepare a product line in 1973 for introduction in 1975.

6 Diversification

	Turnover + £350 Profit + £50	The need for diversification follows from the gap between company objectives (doubling turnover and profits by 1978) and the probable results of the strategies so far thought to be feasible.

Example 2 A manufacturer of sunglasses
Planning period 1973–78 *(cont.)*
Part 3 Action programme for 1973

DEPARTMENT	WORK PROGRAMME
Design	Develop fashion range, with assistance of freelance designer with fashion sense. Prepare trade samples by November. Develop patterns of range of ski-glasses by December. Prepare manufacturing instructions and tools for petrol-station range by March.
Purchasing	Obtain offers and samples for parts for ski-glasses by July. Obtain new plastic forming machine by May in conjunction with production manager.
Administration	Customer accounts and stock records to be carried out by service bureau by May.
Sales	Inform representatives and wholesalers about new conditions. New price lists, including minimum order quantities by February. Complete negotiations with department stores about special sales promoters by April. Sign contract with petrol firm by April. Seek Swedish importer through German Swedish Chamber of Trade and advertisements in Swedish newspapers. Select and sign contract by March. Arrange for market study for ski-glasses in Germany and Austria to be compiled by September. Take stand at Winter Sports Fair 1973.
Personnel	In conjunction with Sales, recruit sales assistant for shop promotions by April. Recruit sales assistant for fashion range by October.
MD's Office	Choose consultant to work on diversification planning by October.

6

Diversification as a marketing strategy

'Diversification' means taking on products for new customers or new applications. By 'extending the product range', we meant retaining the existing customers and applications. A firm undertakes diversification if it takes on products that it has not previously supplied, for the purpose of penetrating new markets or supplying its existing customers with products for new applications.

Diversification can help to achieve the following **objectives** of company planning:

- Spreading the risk, by reducing the company's dependence on a limited number of customers, products or markets.
- Increasing the rate of expansion, if traditional markets are stagnating or only growing very slowly.
- Improving the return on capital, if the return in traditional markets is unsatisfactory.
- Increasing the economic effectiveness of the firm, by providing a more favourable loading for the sales organisation or production capacity.
- Transferring activities into new markets, if all the profit has gone out of the traditional market because of excessive competition or a price collapse.

It must be understood that diversification takes time. From the start of planning a new product to the time when it begins to make a contribution to overheads is usually three to seven years.

Furthermore, the cash position of the firm must be considered. In the early stages of diversification, considerable costs may be incurred for planning, product development, production preparation and introduction to the market. These costs have to be met out of the profits of the current operations of the firm. That can only be done if the new products are got ready before the programme is so obsolete that it is running at a loss.

A representative product life cycle is shown on the next page. It shows how the profits from the traditional products have to cover the costs of the new product in its early stages. This is, however, only a schematic representation. The author's experience shows that there are no general time relationships on which to base long-term predictions about when a market will be saturated and turnover begin to fall. Only through detailed market investigations, taking into account such factors as first purchases, replacement purchases, the competition and technical developments, is it possible to recognise the threat of a downturn in turnover or profits a year or two in advance.

Fig. 6.1 The life cycle of a product

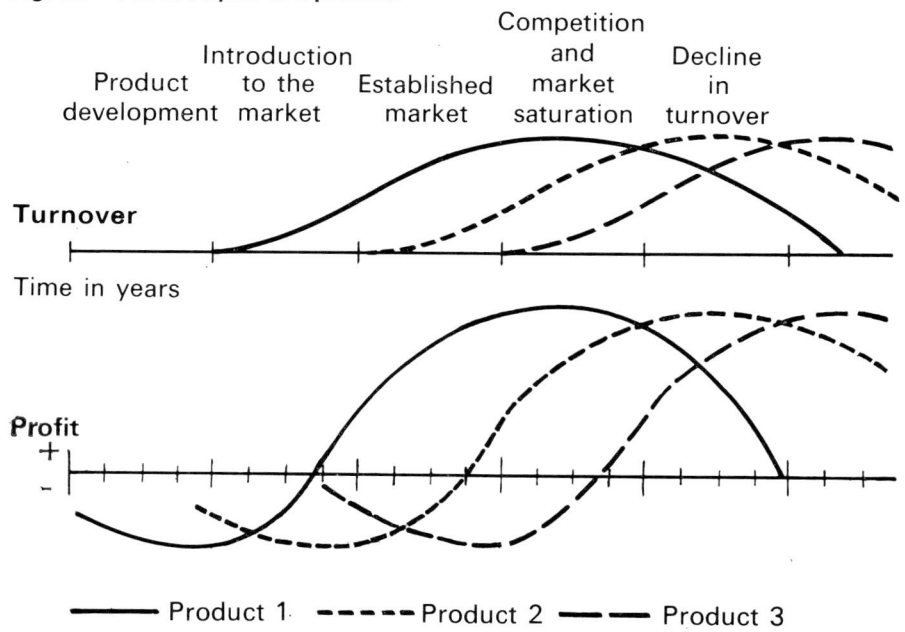

```
                            Competition
         Introduction          and        Decline
Product    to the   Established market      in
development market    market  saturation turnover
```

Turnover

Time in years

Profit

——— Product 1   ----- Product 2   —— — Product 3

Diversification strategies

We can distinguish between horizontal, vertical and lateral diversification strategies. These terms refer to the relationship between the old and the new products and their markets.

Horizontal diversification

New products may be taken on which have close connections with the old products. The connecting link may be the customers, the sales organisation, the applications or the production facilities required.

This has the advantage of limiting the risks of diversification. The firm is not treading wholly new ground. There remain a number of familiar connecting points, from the point of view of the customers, the sales staff or the production technology.

Horizontal diversification

In practice, firms often prefer to start their diversification from their existing customers and sales organisation. In a strongly competitive market, the firm's knowledge of the market and its business connections may make an important contribution towards the successful introduction of a new product. The sales organisation is often the most important asset of a firm embarking on diversification. Such is not the case, however, if diversification is needed because of the falling off of demand among existing customers.

The Bertelsmann group kept to the principle of being true to its market, while systematically diversifying in the leisure market. It originated as a specialist publisher of religious books and then went into specialist and entertainment literature, book clubs, record clubs, printing and schoolbook publishing. The group also produces gramophone records (Ariola), distributes films (Constantin), owns cinemas (UFA) and publishes periodicals (Gruner & Jahr, Heinrich Vogel Verlag). Recently it has extended into remote learning and programmed instruction and the production of TV films and TV cassettes.

The firm of Jungheinrich in Hamburg used to make almost nothing but fork lift trucks and similar vehicles for internal works transport. In 1969 it started making industrial vacuum floor cleaning machines. They could be sold successfully through the intensive sales and service network that had been created for fork lift trucks, and its construction methods and production facilities were also similar.

The firm of Gretsch & Co. in Leonberg, well known in the building industry as manufacturers of building hardware and door fittings, decided to produce ski-bindings. Its purpose was to make itself less dependent on fluctuations in the house-building industry and to create new business in the expanding leisure market. There were close connections between the two product ranges in respect of manufacturing experience, machine tools and production technology. A new sales channel had to be set up to reach the retailers of sports goods.

Unilever, as a large manufacturer of edible fats and washing powders, used its strong sales organisation in the grocery trade to introduce Tree-Top fruit drinks and a range of branded wines called Graf von Bacholsheim, in order to participate in these more strongly growing sectors of the grocery market. There are only limited possibilities of growth in the markets for margarine and washing powders which are dominated by a small number of very large competitors.

In introducing its branded wines in 1970, Unilever was imitating the firm of Allgäuer Alpenmilch. This firm had a strong position in the condensed milk and children's food markets, and in 1965 had added a range of branded wines called Golden October. After taking a long time to get off the ground, the new product-line began to make a contribution to profits in 1969.

SERVICE INSTEAD OF PRODUCTION

A method of diversification that is particularly suitable for smaller firms is to go over from being a manufacturer to being a service business. Medium-sized firms with limited capital resources are often afraid that they may be forced out of business by large competitors, because of being unable to provide the intensive capital investment that may be necessary in their branch of industry to modernise their production facilities.

To go over into the service sector is often a solution to this problem. It avoids the disadvantages of shortage of capital and makes it possible to exploit to the full the firm's close contact with its markets, especially if it is a regional market.

A firm called Rückertshausen in Darmstadt that used to manufacture stoves and cookers under the brand name Rekord has made this transition with great skill. There are many other firms in the field of air-conditioning that used to make ventilators, heat exchangers and ducting, and gradually specialised in the planning, installation and servicing of air-conditioning systems.

A planning section was established first. This could be built on to the existing design office, where there were staff who already knew about air-conditioning technology. At first, the planning was done for a number of fairly simple projects. Later, the installation section of the firm was instructed to install systems that had been planned either inside the firm or by outside consultants.

The proportion of bought-in materials grew, while the components produced in the firm's own factory became a smaller and smaller part of the whole operation. Planning and installation became the dominant activity of the firm. Now, nearly all the machinery is bought from large manufacturers who are able to make pumps, compressors, heat-exchangers, ventilators and similar pieces of apparatus in large quantities and therefore cheaply.

THE 'BAND-WAGON' EFFECT

One of the disadvantages of horizontal diversification, if there is a crisis in that particular branch of industry, is that a number of firms may all have moved over to the same contiguous products; the new market may then suddenly suffer from over supply and a severe price collapse. For example, when the pressure of cheap foreign cloth and the rapid expansion of vertically integrated large firms made things very difficult for many of the smaller companies in the textile industry many textile firms went over to glass fibre fabrics. Large quantities of glass fibre fabrics were offered, competition increased and profits came under severe pressure.

A similar thing happened in the agricultural machinery industry. Many manufacturers of agricultural tractors saw that the market was becoming saturated and started producing small tractor excavators for building sites. This limited market was soon over-supplied and the profits of firms involved in it were seriously threatened.

Vertical diversification

Vertical diversification consists of taking on products that occur prior to or

Vertical diversification

subsequent to the traditional products of the firm. In practice, it is nearly always subsequent products that are considered. Prior markets seldom offer favourable conditions for diversification: substantially higher capital investment is usually needed to enter a market for raw materials or semi-finished goods, than is required at the conversion stage. Furthermore, the firm's competitors would have to be approached as customers, a situation which often prejudices the chances of success. Above all, it is not usually possible to exert any significant influence on the application or sales of the end product through the medium of the prior products. However, that does not mean the the prior product areas are of no importance at all for company planning, since the purpose of entering the prior areas is not normally diversification, but securing the firm's supply of raw materials on favourable terms.

European steel producers have opened up ore deposits in Africa, and the Japanese have become actively engaged in mining businesses in South America and Australia.

On the other hand, the three leading German chemical firms, BASF, Farbwerke Hoechst and Farbenfabriken Bayer, have shown a pronounced inclination towards vertical diversification downwards. BASF, the successor to IG Farben in heavy chemicals, has successfully entered various subsequent product areas such as paints and varnishes, manmade fibres, pharmaceutical products and magnetic tapes. As a result of this policy, BASF is today not only a manufacturer of heavy chemicals and synthetic materials, but also produces finished products.

Vertical diversification offers the possibility of substantially increasing the 'value added' within the firm and thus improving the returns. It is particularly significant that the final conversion stage is the place where the sales and applications of the products in question can be directly influenced. Thus BASF can promote the sales of raw materials for paints and varnishes by developing better varnishes for the motor-car industry or intensifying its sales of paints and varnishes to the building industry.

Waldhof in Mannheim, originally a paper mill, entered the conversion field in spite of severe foreign competition in order to compensate for steadily increasing raw materials and wages costs. The firm now makes paper sacks, corrugated paper, handkerchiefs, nappies, toilet paper and cellulose wadding. The household paper products are sold through the grocery trade under the brand name Zewa.

Schwäbische Hüttenwerke, an iron and steel works in Wasseralfingen, had to transform itself into an engineering firm when its ore reserves in South Germany gave out. The restructuring of the company began by extending its steel-forming and -casting activities. Machine construction already represents about 30 per cent of turnover: machine tools, machine parts, rollers and gear-trains. The next objective is to build up the technology of materials handling (eccentric helical pumps) in order to secure its position in the market by offering increasingly sophisticated products.

If a policy of vertical integration is followed, the later more sophisticated products must show a satisfactory profitability on their own merits alone. The benefits of having the converting stages as a captive market for the firm's own raw materials are not usually so overwhelming that it is possible to dispense with a proper return from them.

Firms producing raw materials or semi-finished products, who are considering vertical diversification, must remember that they will be competing with their own long-standing customers. The latter may take umbrage and transfer their custom elsewhere. Experience shows, however, that the reaction of customers to competition from their suppliers varies very widely from industry to industry, and vertical diversification should be investigated by market research, so that the effect on turnover in the traditional areas can be estimated.

Lateral diversification

Diversification without any connection at all between the traditional areas and the proposed new markets is known as 'lateral diversification'. The firm moves into a new unfamiliar area, without relying on links with its previous activities, and therefore without relying on the support of an existing sales organisation, existing business connections or existing technical know-how. The decisive criterion for lateral diversification is therefore the expected return on capital.

An example of this is Böhler & Weber, an Augsburg firm, which was well known for a very long time as a manufacturer of machines for laundries and dry cleaners. For some years, it has also been making ancillary machines for data-processing installations, such as automatic guillotines, folders and collators, in order to participate in the dynamic computer market. Since 1964 it has also made automatic washing machines.

The German Babcock & Wilcox firm in Oberhausen has also committed itself to lateral diversification. The management recognised as early as 1960 that boiler-making, which then accounted for 85 per cent of the turnover, could not promise the desired rate of growth. The main reasons were the trend towards larger units and the transition from coal to nuclear power. A forward strategy was worked out with the purpose of moving into growth industries, without neglecting their power station business. Takeovers were the main instrument of business policy. By 1969, the total turnover was made up as follows: power station products, 37 per cent; industrial installations, machine construction and building, 32 per cent; wholesale and retail trade (electrical goods, supermarkets and discount stores), 31 per cent. The acquisitions of the firm in recent years include five firms in the air-drying and air-conditioning field, one each in materials handling, acid protection, heat exchangers, machine tools and plastic moulding, and four firms in the wholesale and retail trade.

The financial resources for this expansion came from the cashflow in the traditional areas and the issue of new shares. The traditional areas of the firm also contributed to the general diversification by going into garbage incinerators, fittings and the building trade.

THE CONGLOMERATE

Lateral diversification on a large scale, and in several different areas simultaneously, transforms the specialist firm into a mixed concern or conglomerate, characterised by widely diversified activities in totally different industries. The subsidiaries often operate as quasi-independent firms, controlled by the central administration. Modern conglomerates are often based on the purchase of existing firms by share-exchanges and intensive cultivation of the stock markets to achieve high P/E ratios for the shares.

The American conglomerate International Telephone and Telegraph Company (ITT) is an example of rapid growth by lateral diversification and acquisitions. It doubled its turnover and profits within five years.

The firm originally operated telephone systems in South America and Europe and manufactured telephone equipment and radios. There were only limited opportunities for growth in this market. In 1959, the firm decided to seek new markets with better prospects of expansion. The firm became particularly interested in the service sector, because the opportunities for growth in this area are favourable, and service firms can usually be acquired more cheaply (in terms of the P/E ratio) than, for example, electronics or pharmaceutical firms.

Between 1960 and 1965, the acquisitions included AVIS car hire, an insurance company, an investment company, and a bank. In 1968 and 1969, the tempo of the takeovers increased. The six biggest acquisitions, Sheraton Hotels, a construction company, a paper mill, a grocery firm, an engineering firm and a firm making vending machines increased the turnover by over £700 million and the profits by over £20 million. ITT also owns several European firms. These acquisitions were financed almost exclusively by issuing shares and preference shares.

ITT is the prototype of the successful multinational conglomerate. In 1969, the total turnover of £1,200 million came 65 per cent from North America and 53 per cent from overseas, mainly Europe. The fact that of the total profit of £97·5 million, 55 per cent was earned in North America and 45 per cent overseas seems to show that it is easier to make profits outside the USA.

ITT maintains a large staff division in its administrative offices in Brussels and New York that is constantly on the lookout for suitable firms to buy.

ACQUISITION OF 'SLEEPERS'

The diversification policies of the aggressive conglomerates include the purchase of so-called 'sleepers', that is, firms that are earning low profits because of an inactive management and can therefore be taken over cheaply. After the takeover, the management is reorganised and stimulated to perform better. If necessary, a special 'commando' from headquarters is provided.

Conglomerates have many similarities with an industrial bank. Control of the member companies is exercised principally through financial and accounting systems with the aid of cunningly devised budgets. But there is one essential difference: the management of the conglomerate does not confine itself to financial control of the firms that have been taken over, but exercises an active influence on the conduct of the business in order to increase turnover, earnings and profit per share. The turnover of AVIS in 1965, when it was taken over by ITT, was nearly £20 million and the profit over £1 million. By 1969, the turnover had risen to over £80 million and the profit to £3.7 million.

The parent company's expertise in the fields of marketing, production, development and finance is available to the subsidiaries. The conglomerate invests not only capital, but also management know-how in order to increase the return on its participation. To do this, the management of the conglomerate must have at its disposal a sufficient number of competent managers whom it can put into the firms it has taken over when this is necessary. This means, in turn, that the conglomerate has a strong interest in retaining experienced managers in the firms it has acquired and binding them to itself after the takeover. Share options and profit-sharing schemes have a special part to play. An attractive personnel policy is an important condition for the long-term success of a conglomerate.

Organisation and personnel considerations are important everywhere, not merely in conglomerates. In a small firm that is trying to establish a second string, success may depend on clear organisation and a sensible definition of the tasks and obligations of each manager, as well as on the delegation of responsibilities. The type of boss of a firm who makes all the decisions himself will not be competent to cope with diversification. He will be quickly overwhelmed by a flood of details, plans and decisions.

Sources of ideas for diversification

In order to carry out systematic product planning, the firm needs to assemble a fairly large but manageable collection of product proposals. This gives a reasonable chance that a product suited to the firm will be selected at the end of the process of critical examination. The assembled proposals should, however, all be suitable in principle for the diversification objectives of the firm. This means that products must satisfy conditions that have been laid down as essential objectives at the start of the process of diversification planning.

In order to set up a reasonable number of basically suitable product-candidates (in practice about ten or twenty) the firm should activate as many sources of ideas for products as possible, both internal and external to the company.

Having made a short list of suitable projects, attention can be concentrated on what appear to be the most suitable. Such product proposals are not usually genuine new developments, such as lasers or hovercraft, but are products already accepted by the market or product improvements. Experience shows that new inventions are loaded with too much risk for the purposes of diversification, because it is easy to underestimate the time and money that will be needed to bring an invention to the market. The enthusiastic inventor and tinkerer who persuades the diversification-minded management to put his discovery on the market all too often brings the firm nothing but bitter disappointments and serious cash problems.

A product selected for diversification should be at the beginning of a phase of market expansion, as were deep freezers, car safety belts and vending machines a few years ago. These were products that had been known in principle for many years, but it was a long time before technical and economic developments provided the right conditions for expansive growth.

Intuitive considerations

An important and readily accessible source of product proposals is formed by the members of the senior management and staff sections of the firm. This circle of people is familiar with the objectives of the proposed diversification and directly interested in its success.

The quality of the proposals that come forward from this group is in practice mostly very high. But they must be given time to develop their proposals. Creativity cannot be forced under pressure of time. It is therefore advisable to inform the members of the senior management, the sales management and the staff sections as early as possible and to remind them regularly that product proposals are expected from them. Chance observations, suggestions arising from professional contacts and ideas occurring spontaneously have often led to useful proposals. People should be encouraged to keep notebooks and enter brief reminders of their ideas so that they are not lost. After a time, such notebooks can become rich sources of good ideas.

Observing the rest of industry

Useful suggestions for new products can be gained by observing the competitors. Consciously or unconsciously, everybody concerned with new product planning does this. The object is to discover what new products are being put on the market by the leading competitors, at home and above all in export markets. Annual reports, Press releases, articles in technical journals, exhibitions, etc., can provide information about products that have attracted special attention by the competitors or by the customers.

The author's experience shows that for European firms such 'industry investigations' are particularly fruitful in the US market. Large American firms are in the habit of talking very freely about their product developments and diversification policies. The study of their annual reports and technical discussions with their planning experts provide useful leads and also contacts that can be directly exploited for licensing purposes.

These searches are often carried out under the assumption that what is on the market in America today will be in demand in European markets in a few years' time. This is certainly a very suggestive way of looking at things. But the dangers of uncritically transferring American market conditions to Europe must be recognised. For example, over a million domestic air-conditioners are sold annually in the USA but comparable sales could never be achieved in Europe. Similarly, with deep-frozen 'TV meals'. Careful market research must be carried out in order to discover whether the conditions in the US market can be transferred to the European firm and its market.

Brainstorming

Brainstorming is thinking aloud in a group of about eight to twelve people. The participants discuss a problem among themselves and develop proposals for solving it.

The leader of the group should present the problem in as general a form as possible, so as not to limit unnecessarily the scope of the participants' suggestions. If the discussion stagnates or becomes one-sided, he has to reactivate it and set it on the desired lines again.

It is important for the success of a brainstorming session that the ideas put forward by the participants should not be criticised at the session. All ideas should be taken up, however impractical or unrealistic they may seem. The critical examination and selection is carried out later by the specialists in the planning section.

In the author's experience, the advantages of brainstorming lie more on the quantitative than on the qualitative side. But the very multiplicity of ideas generates a certain likelihood that unexpected suggestions will come up, well away from the accustomed habits in the company, that would not have been discovered by systematic methods.

A brainstorming session lasts about two hours. It is a cheap way of collecting suggestions from colleagues and business friends. A further advantage is that the staff get the feeling that their suggestions are valued highly by the senior executives. This leads to a positive attitude later, when plans are being implemented.

Functional analysis

This is an important procedure for the systematic development of product ideas. The firm must first decide which customers it wants to supply. A particular market might be chosen as the target because the firm happens to have suitable sales channels for it.

A functional analysis then starts from the tasks that the customer has to perform when carrying out his activities. The object is to work out 'solutions to problems'

Functional analysis

and then to offer them for sale in the form of a product, a machine or a service. The investigation is centred on the question:

- What tasks does my future customer have to perform, and how can I as a supplier help him to simplify them?

The customer's workflow is systematically analysed, by methods similar to those used for analysing an existing materials-flow. Functional analysis is particularly useful to the manufacturer of capital goods. As the decision to buy machines is dominated by economic considerations, a piece of equipment that saves costs can be relied on to produce a demand for itself.

An important consideration relating to functional analyses of capital goods is the long-term increase in wage costs by more than 6 per cent per year and the increasing shortage of skilled labour in the long term due to the demographic structure of the population. It is therefore important to calculate the payback on a new machine at the present wage level, and then at the prospective wage level in five years' time (35–50 per cent higher) and in ten years' time (80–120 per cent higher).

Economic forecasts of this kind, carried out, for example, with reference to the introduction of numerical controls for machine tools, show that the expected rise in wage costs will make certain types of machine uneconomic within a few years, and will create a demand for new processes and machines.

7

Ways of implementing an expansion programme

To implement its marketing plan a firm can:

- Develop its own products and expand its own sales organisation;
- Take out licences;
- Create subsidiaries jointly with other firms (joint ventures);
- Purchase existing firms.

Depending on the choice of market objectives, different methods of expansion are appropriate for different purposes. For example, a given firm wishing to increase its share of its own market might best achieve this by doing its own development work, while diversification might be more easily achieved by taking out licences or buying an existing firm. In another case, it might be easier and more profitable to increase the firm's share of the market by buying a competitor, rather than trying to increase its turnover by its own efforts.

Which of the above methods is the most suitable must be decided in each case by careful examination of the market circumstances, the capital requirements and the prospective returns. The choice of the most suitable method of expansion is one of the tasks of company planning. It is especially important if the marketing plan has as its objective either rapid expansion in the present market or diversification.

Product and sales development within the firm

Under this method, the firm itself creates the technical and sales conditions for realising its market objectives. Capital has to be invested in the form of development costs and the costs of building up a sales organisation. Doing the development work oneself has the advantage that the firm itself can decide exactly what features the product shall have, how many sales offices shall be opened, and so

Product and sales development within the firm 65

on. The objectives can be laid down exactly and the know-how and experience gained during the development work benefits the firm's own staff and can form the basis for further expansion. This is particularly important with products that are in a state of rapid technical development. One learns from one's own mistakes, and one does better next time.

An important disadvantage is the fact that the cost in time and money of reaching the target cannot be reliably known in advance. Exceeding the original cost estimates is a way of seriously endangering the profitability of a new project. The staff of research and development departments always underestimate the time needed and the cost of getting a new product ready for the market. The cause of this is not merely optimism and pride, but often political tactics as well: consciously or unconsciously, the spiritual fathers of a project always act on the well-established principle that a low cost estimate will have a favourable effect on the decision to develop a product inside the firm. Once the decision has been taken and development costs have been incurred, the management seldom has the strength of will to wind up the project. Afterwards, hardly anyone ever asks who made the original cost estimates.

Military development projects are a good example of this phenomenon. The cost of the American Galaxy Transport aircraft was originally estimated at £7 million each. The actual cost was £17 million. The MBT 70 tank that was to be developed jointly by the German and US Armies had a similar history. The development costs were originally estimated at £40 million. When they had reached the figure of £200 million the project was discontinued. In spite of being four years late, there were still a large number of unsolved problems.

Political considerations play a large part in military projects. Someone wants a new weapon system and knows that a parliament is much more likely to authorise the expenditure if the cost estimates are low.

The case is often much the same with civil projects financed by the State. The development costs of Concorde, the supersonic aircraft, were estimated in 1962 at £150 million. The revised estimate announced in September 1970 was £730 million, and in May 1972, £970 million with an official indication that the final development costs might exceed £1 000 million. The Olympic Games at Munich in 1972 show a similar history of low initial cost estimates which were dwarfed by the actual performance.

In a firm there is a similar play of interests between the technical development people on the one side and the company management on the other.

Apart from such technical questions, the technical problems that will occur during the development of new projects cannot usually be anticipated with sufficient accuracy. While the development is going on, the competitive situation or the demands of the market may change, so that product changes are forced on the firm for which no one is to blame, and the original time and cost estimates are heavily exceeded.

Such surprises are not confined to technical development work. When building up a sales organisation, unpleasant surprises can happen again and again, especially if one is opening up a foreign country or an unfamiliar market. Forecasts about the scale and tempo of market penetration, no matter how many calculations have been carried out by the market research people, are only estimates based on a large number of assumptions. The estimate is only as good as the market research man's judgment. Unpredicted and unpredictable problems can arise: the newly appointed sales manager hands in his resignation, the competitor lowers his prices, and retail outlets are hesitant about putting the new product on their shelves.

The risks of development within the firm are demonstrated by the attempt of the firm of J. Eckes to enter the market for freeze-dried foods. This firm had introduced a fruit drink called High C in Germany with great dynamism and skill and had also won an important share of the market for alcoholic drinks. The firm wished to diversify, and to use for this purpose a newly licensed process of spray drying together with its own sales force which was well introduced in the grocery trade.

Market investigations carried out by the firm showed that there was a demand for dried soft cheese, mashed potato and similar convenience products. At first, the preparations went according to plan. But then there were technical troubles in operating the spray drying process which were the more difficult to deal with because the firm had no experience in the field of food manufacture. Furthermore, the sales representatives were less successful with the large grocery outlets than had been expected because the buyers who dealt with cheese and mashed potato were not the same people as those who bought fruit juices. The consequence was that operating costs were far above the planned figure and sales developed more slowly than had been planned. The project had to be terminated. The spray drying machine which had been installed at great expense was sold.

The further a firm penetrates into unfamiliar territories on either the technical or the sales side, the greater is the uncertainty attaching to cost estimates and the higher the risk. This can, however, be limited by regular project reviews, as is described in detail in chapter 10, 'Product Planning'.

If a project has to be abandoned because the original time and cost estimates have proved to be unrealistic, substantial financial losses will be incurred. The lost time may be even more serious, if the purpose was to provide a successor for a dying product-line or an alternative to a stagnating sales channel. The firm's efforts to provide new products have now been delayed by the corresponding amount of time, and it may now be too late to bring another product to point of yielding profits in time. Money can be replaced, but time can never be bought back.

If diversification is the objective, the decision to open up a new market out of the firm's own resources should only be taken after carefully weighing up the strengths of the firm and comparing them critically with the advantages and disadvantages of producing under licence, of forming a joint venture, and of acquiring another firm.

Licences and selling rights

Their advantage is that the costs of bringing the product on to the market are more accurately predictable and the timespan usually shorter. This means a reduced risk.

All the same, licences and selling rights must be carefully checked before they are taken out, to ensure that local conditions are suitable for a successful sales effort. Even if a product is successful in the USA the market potential and the technical demands of the European market may be completely different. Many firms have lived to regret taking out a licence in too much of a hurry without first testing the market. A well-known German producer of electrical goods took out an American licence for domestic air-conditioners. About three million a year are sold in the USA, but very few were sold in Germany, in spite of intensive advertising.

There were several reasons. The European climate is not such as to make air-conditioning in private houses essential, even where a high degree of comfort is required, so that the market that bought air-conditioners in the USA does not do so in Europe. Building practices were another obstacle. In USA sash windows are nearly always used, which make the installation of the air-conditioners very simple. In most European countries casement windows are normal, which do not allow the air-conditioner to be mounted in the window frame, and structural alterations are therefore needed. For these reasons, the expectations of German importers and producers of air conditioners have always been disappointed.

Almost every product introduced from abroad has to have its mode of operating or its appearance changed in order to conform to consumer habits, legal requirements or technical standards in European markets. These changes can be quite costly and can make the value of a licence questionable.

The choice between taking out a licence and developing within the firm must also take into account the imposition of licence fees. Products that are expected to be affected by severe price competition in the future may have their profitability seriously threatened by licence fees. The usual fee of between 3 per cent and 7 per cent may take the lion's share of the firm's profit margin.

Taking out a licence involves much more than a legal agreement, giving the right to use brand names and patents. The licencee also needs to be continuously supported by his partner with know-how and advice. In practice, this demands the fullest exchange of ideas and close personal contact between managers from the two sides responsible for design, production, sales and technical service. This is a matter of decisive importance if the product has to be modified to suit the local manufacturing and market conditions.

In the case of products that are open to continuous further development, access to the results of future development work of the licensor is of vital importance, if the licensee is to maintain his own competitive position and protect his investment in sales and production facilities. Here, too, the closest personal contact is needed and there must be a constant exchange of experience.

Licences create rights *sui generis*. Disputes cannot be settled by general conditions as in labour law or tenancies. Hence, before signing a licence contract, it is highly advisable to run through all future eventualities and think out their consequences, so that as far as possible all foreseeable developments are contractually regulated and disputes thus avoided. Checklist 7 gives a list of points that need to be thought about.

Taking out a licence is only one among several means of reaching a given marketing objective. Before taking out a licence, a firm should check carefully whether it offers real advantages over development within the firm, a joint venture, or buying another firm.

Checklist 7 Licensing contracts

1 Market research: investigate the sales opportunities for the product and the technical demands of the market before signing the contract: it often happens that technical changes have to be made in the product, to make it suitable for the home market.

2 What the licensor has to provide: patent rights, know-how (design, production, sales), drawings, tools, brand markings, advertising.

3 Duration of the contract and of the payment of royalties; arrangements for terminating the contract.

4 Reduction or cancellation of royalties if a patent or part-patent expires or is declared void.

5 Premature termination of the contract if the product does not sell or is rendered obsolete by technical developments.

6 Defence of patents: who must take the legal action and bear the costs?

7 Product improvements by the licensor: the licensee's rights.

8 Product improvements and improvements in the production process by the licensee: effect on royalties; what development costs are borne by the licensor?

9 Delimitation of licensor's and licensee's markets, rules relating to export and re-export; transfer of existing customers from the licensor to the licensee.

10 Delimitation in respect of other future licensees in other countries. (The EEC rules on cartels make this increasingly difficult.)

11 Issue of licences or know-how to third parties. Issue of sublicences. Cross-licensing agreements with business partners of the licensee. Incorporation of parts or subassemblies made under licence in products other than those envisaged in the agreement.

12 Manufacture or sale of competing products by the licensee.

13 Methods of calculation of royalties and time when they fall due: on production, on being sold, or on reaching an agreed turnover?

14 Evidence and documentation of production, sales or turnover.

15 Quality control by the licensor; agreements about taking samples, approving the production process or the factory.

16 Agreement about legal obligation for the product and defence against customer claims under consumer protection.

17 Deduction of taxes from royalties. Obtaining the necessary currency permits.

18 Defence against cartel legislation. Costs of cartel proceedings. Changes in the agreement if important conditions are disallowed. (Especially important because the EEC market has a rather strong anti-trust legislation which might render sales protection clauses between licensor and licensee void.)

19 Period of protection: embargo on production and sales after the expiration of the contract.

20 Agreement about an arbitrator in case of difficulties.

Joint ventures

A joint venture implies a much more intensive relation between the licensor and the licensee than in the case of a licence contract. Both firms are affected strongly by the success or failure of the joint subsidiary. Very often in practice it is an indigenous firm and a foreign firm that combine in this way. The foreign firm brings its production know-how and patents into the country and the local firm provides knowledge of the market or a sales organisation.

A joint venture is often more effective than a licensing arrangement in circumstances where success in a new market depends on close and lasting exchanges of experience and personal contact. The transfer of experience in development, production, sales and technical service takes up a great deal of the licensor's management time, and while they are doing this they are not available for their normal duties in the parent companies.

A licensee can be severely harmed and can be forced to incur unnecessarily high preparation costs by the unwillingness of his licensor to provide the time to make his experience available. Many a hope of profit from a licensed product has had to be buried because of the licensor being slow to answer questions and unwilling to cooperate in resolving unexpected problems.

If the licensor is participating in the investment and the future profits, the necessary sacrifices come more easily. 'If my money is in it, so is my heart.'

A joint venture has the disadvantage that each parent firm can only partially influence the policies of the subsidiary and is dependent on its partner. The close personal contact brings the risk of personality difficulties if the managers from the two participating firms do not get on. A successful joint venture can only be founded on mutual confidence. Unforeseen difficulties and setbacks occur especially during the preparatory phase of a joint venture and place a strain on the personal relationships of its partners.

Partners in a joint venture may in fact have opposing long-range business interests which make the venture problematic. It often happens that one partner is following a static business policy with the objective of reaching a certain limit of turnover and drawing off the profits that arise at that level. The other partner may want to force an expansion of the market by reinvesting the profits and additional capital. A joint venture may also be regarded by one partner as the first step towards participation in the other, with the objective of eventually buying him out completely. Hence, it is very important to clarify the interests and long-term intentions of both partners before signing a partnership agreement.

Buying existing firms

A firm may be bought with the object of incorporating it with the parent company, or of operating it as a subsidiary company. Takeovers as a means of expansion have the advantage that a substantial increase in turnover and profit can be achieved in a very short time.

Company acquisition is also the means of expansion where the risk associated with entering on new activities or new markets is most accurately predictable.

A firm that is considered for takeover usually has long years of experience in its market. The current profitability can be checked from the company's books, and future returns can be assessed with sufficient accuracy by investigations into the market and the company.

For these reasons, takeovers are nowadays the preferred method of penetrating new markets. In 1964, Dupont took over the old Frankfurt photographic firm of Adox-Schleussner-Werke. The American firm of Koehring Company, manufacturers of machines for the building industry, bought itself into the German market by taking over the Hamburg firm of excavator manufacturers called Menck and Hambrock. Large German chemical firms such as BASF, Farbwerke Hoechst and Bayer have built up their market positions in paints, synthetic materials and pharmaceuticals by takeovers. At the end of 1969, Bayer bought the American Wyandotte Chemical Corporation in order to get into the American market for heavy chemicals. In 1970, Farbwerke Hoechst bought the English paint firm of Berger.

Buying a firm is a good way of achieving the following **growth objectives**:

- Increasing the market share in the traditional market by buying a competitor and taking over his customers, sales organisation and production capacity.
- Acquiring a sales organisation in order to sell the products of the firm in other countries.
- Penetrating a new market (diversification) by acquiring products, know-how, production experience, market knowledge and a sales organisation.

As a means of diversification, the purchase of another company offers the following **advantages**:

- Penetration of the desired new market is accelerated. The firm to be acquired should therefore have experienced managers, well-introduced products and an effective sales organisation, so that the cost in time and money of developing products and sales organisation can be saved.
- The risk that is unavoidably associated with opening up new markets and developing new products is greatly reduced and becomes largely predictable, because the current rates of profit and the information needed to assess the likely future trend of profits can usually be established with sufficient accuracy from the records of the firm that is to be bought.

All the same, mistakes are frequent in the acquisition of firms. It is often done too hastily, and on the basis of an overestimate of the advantages and underestimate of the difficulties of integrating the acquisition into the parent firm.

The purchase of the German radio and television manufacturer Kuba-Imperial by the American General Electric in 1966 is a good example of an acquisition

Buying existing firms

that went wrong. General Electric is alleged to have paid the sole owner of Kuba, Herr Gerhard Kubetschek, some £10 million for his company. The takeover happened while black and white TV sales were still in full flood. Shortly afterwards the market began to be affected by colour TV. Later, there were difficulties about price policies, and on the production side quality problems with colour TV sets began to arise in the Kuba factories.

After trying for several years to increase the sales and profits of Kuba, General Electric gave up the attempt and sold Kuba to AEG Telefunken. People in the know maintain that General Electric received about £6 or £7 million in AEG shares, at their market price. If that is true, General Electric lost £3 or £4 million on the deal, in addition to heavy operating losses during its period of ownership. The main causes of the loss were: the difficulties of the German radio and TV market were seriously underestimated, and the potential for improving the situation by putting in a new management was greatly overestimated. In 1972, AEG realised that it could not solve Kuba's problems and closed down the firm's main plant.

The precondition for a successful acquisition is to decide clearly in advance of the purchase exactly what objectives it is designed to achieve. Is it only to obtain a competitor's share of the market? Is it to obtain a new product-range, to be incorporated in one's own production programmes, in order to save the development costs? Is it to obtain a going sales organisation? Is it to obtain extra production capacity? Is it to obtain a management team that the parent firm needs in order to achieve its objectives?

These questions must be answered very carefully. On the answer depends whether it is at all possible for the takeover of a candidate to be successful, and whether the price is justified.

MANAGEMENT IS THE MOST IMPORTANT ASSET TO BE ACQUIRED

Especially if the object of the takeover is diversification, the quality and number of the managers in the firm that is to be purchased are a very important consideration. Only if these assets can be integrated into the parent firm is the purchase likely to be worth while in the long run.

The management structure of the proposed acquisition should therefore be carefully assessed. Private firms with less than 1000 employees usually have too narrow and too shallow a management structure. The owner is often the only senior executive. The senior foreman, the chief bookkeeper and chief salesman are directly responsible to him. In firms of this kind, the few members of the middle management are often unable to carry out the functions of the owner and keep the firm going; expansion is quite out of their reach. If the owner leaves, the firm loses its know-how, its knowledge of the product and the production processes, its market experience and its customer contacts. After the owner has received his money, it is to be expected that he will wish to free himself from the troubles of active management and leave. This can seriously endanger the success of the purchase. When an acquisition is being considered it is most important to think out very carefully what would be the effect of the loss of one or more of the senior executives of the firm. It must be expected in practice that takeovers will always lead to tension and personality difficulties, which will cause some of the former managers to leave. The effect of their leaving depends on the objectives of the purchase. If the objective was simply additional production capacity, their loss may not be too serious. If the objective was to enter a new market and then expand, the loss of important executives could seriously threaten the success of the takeover.

This was what the American washing-machine firm Maytag found when they took over the Wuppertal firm of Hohmann-Werke, manufacturers of stoves, cookers and washing machines, in order to get a foot in Europe. Herr Hohmann had built up his firm with great skill. The purchase contract provided for him to remain as General Manager. A few months later he died from a heart attack.

Maytag found that they could not run the firm successfully with the existing middle management. Maytag managers sent over from the USA were not at home in the unfamiliar European market. The result was that in the ensuing phase of concentration and price reduction in the market for household goods, Hohmann–Maytag was unable to maintain its position. A few years later, the firm which had been bought with such optimistic hopes had to be wound up.

The lesson to be learnt from experiences of this kind is as follows:

- Many firms with less than 1000 employees have so thin a management structure that the loss of the owner and one or two executives in key positions can reduce the firm to not being able to continue operating. Therefore, it often does not make sense to buy a medium-sized firm for purposes of diversification and entering new markets. Because the firm making the purchase has to be considerably bigger than the firm being bought, it follows that takeovers are a practicable means of diversification or entering new markets only for very large firms. For smaller firms, takeovers are for the most part only suitable for expanding in the buyer's existing market by acquiring additional production capacity or market share. In this case, the firm making the purchase usually has enough knowledge of the production process and the market to make good the loss of a few senior executives.

The purchase price formulae for valuing a firm are useless

The parent firm must get an adequate return from its purchase. Hence, the importance of establishing the maximum purchase price that is acceptable. There is strong competition in the market for firms, especially from foreign and, above all, American purchasers. In the present period of concentration and diversification, high prices are demanded for well-managed firms, which may be of the order of eight to twenty times the annual earnings after tax, or even more. But there is no point whatever in making a purchase unless the buyer can achieve thereby a good return on capital. If the price is based on a ratio of

The purchase price formulae for valuing a firm are useless

twenty to one, an adequate return is only possible if a strong integration effect can be achieved, on the principle that 1 + 1 = 3. Such an integration effect can be brought about in the form of cost reduction in both firms as a consequence of combining their operations, or where the integration opens up new sales channels for both firms, or by forced expansion of the firm that has been taken over. The last, however, requires still more capital.

The integration effect determines the value of the firm

Before a purchase is made, the nature and scale of the integration effect must be carefully investigated, because this is what fixes the maximum price that is worth paying for the firm.

The maximum acceptable price cannot be established by a firm of certified public accountants or any other 'neutral' advisers. For purposes of planning the return on capital to be achieved by the purchase, the following factors must be taken into effect in establishing the maximum price that can be justified:

- Asset value
- Value of earnings (P/E ratio)
- Value of the integration effect.

The past values of the first two can be discovered by examining the firm's accounts. These are only historical values which as a rule only serve to fix a minimum price from the point of view of the seller. Much more important is future profits, and they can only be estimated if adequate information can be extracted about the future development of the market, the position of the firm in its market and the competitive situation and price conditions. The same considerations must be taken into account as have already been described in the chapter on company appraisal (chapter 2). It is obvious that external accountants who must base their report principally on historical bookkeeping figures have little to contribute to the estimation of future profits.

It is even more difficult to estimate the value of the future integration effect. The present cost structures and the future organisation of both firms have to be investigated and, if necessary, replanned. One has to find out whether particular areas of the two firms, such as production, sales or administration, can be combined and what cost advantages would ensue.

It is important to realise that the integration effect can only be achieved if the planned integration can, in fact, be carried out. This part of the purchase price investigation therefore always involves a substantial element of risk.

Planning the return on capital plays a decisive part in takeovers. The buyer must take care not to water down the return on capital of the parent firm by paying an excessive price. This danger is always present if the purchase price represents a high P/E ratio, because of the risk of being unable to implement the planned integration effects.

In limited companies, it is of no consequence from the point of view of return on capital whether the price is paid in cash, by exchange of shares or by issuing new shares, so long as the firm has access to the capital market. If an exchange of shares takes place or the purchase is financed by issuing new shares at the current market value, the shareholder's return on capital is not endangered so long as the ratio of the market price of the parent company's shares to its profit per share (P/E ratio) is higher than that represented by the purchase price of the firm that is being taken over. So long as this condition is satisfied, there is no watering down of the return on the parent company's shares.

The policy of buying firms at a lower P/E ratio than that of the parent firm's shares is the basis of the American conglomerates' planning. This presupposes that the shares of the parent company have a higher than average P/E ratio.

German firms have sometimes succeeded in financing their takeovers by issuing new shares. The price that BASF paid in 1968 for the paint manufacturer Herbol corresponded to a P/E ratio of 19. The purchase price for the pharmaceutical firm of Nordmark-Werke was 16 at a time when BASF shares had a P/E ratio of about 18. The BASF shareholders thus got the full benefit of the integration effects of taking over Herbol and Nordmark.

A favourable opportunity for getting substantial returns from a takeover is offered by the purchase of so called 'sleepers'. These are firms that have a poor reputation on the stock market due to a weak management, or that have a low P/E ratio because of a temporary setback in profits, and whose owners are willing to sell at a low price (in P/E terms).

Their asset value and the value of their earnings is usually low. If they are making losses, one cannot speak of earnings value at all.

If the buyer is able to reactivate the firm and, if necessary, supply it with a new management, he gets the full benefit of any increase in profits. In the case of sleepers, the integration effect is usually fairly easy to achieve if it is a firm in the same or related industry, so that production and sales can be wholly or partly combined with the parent firm.

Thyssen-Bornemisza tried to swallow up a sleeper in 1965 by buying the once well-known firm of Pintsch-Bamag. The Thyssen experts believed that this family firm, which was operating at a loss, could be turned into a profitable member of the diversification-happy group if it were bought cheaply and the works management modernised.

But they had underestimated Pintsch-Bamag's difficulties and overestimated the capacity of the new management. In spite of optimistic forecasts, they did not succeed in tightening up the firm's production programme and rationalising its methods sufficiently. Although the previous year's turnover was exceeded by 40 per cent in the boom year of 1969, the losses reached dizzy heights.

In addition to the purchase price of £3 million, the group had to pay out nearly £10 million to cover losses over the first four years, whereas a commitment of only about £5 million in total had been anticipated. When the total commitment had reached some £13 million the group remembered the old rule about not throwing good money after bad. The subsidiary that had been acquired with such high hopes was dropped, and had to go into liquidation. Suppliers, ordinary shareholders and pensioners got 35 per cent of their claims.

At the last annual meeting of the dying firm, the Board stated laconically: 'the structural problem of Pintsch-Bamag was recognised in its full extent only at the end of 1969'. One shareholder said out loud what everyone was thinking. 'Herr Baron, you must have had some dreadful advisers at that time. You have been duped.'

The Pintsch-Bamag episode shows that the old Roman trader's saying *caveat emptor* (let the buyer beware) applies quite particularly to the buying of firms.

The two chemical giants BASF and Dow Chemical had to learn by bitter experience that buying firms is not a royal road to profits.

These two experienced chemical firms wanted to go into the expanding manmade fibres market together by taking over Phrix. But they had miscalculated: Phrix was active mainly in rayon and cellulose. Fully manmade fibres, which promised so much for the future, made up only a small part of Phrix's turnover. But as there was a price collapse in cellulose fibres, Phrix sank further and further into the red.

By 1966, the acquisition had cost BASF nearly £40 million in purchase price, losses and further investment. The operating loss for 1969 was about £10 million. BASF and Dow then decided to order a slimming cure for their daughter in Hamburg. Several of the Phrix factories were closed and the firm's level of activity was sharply cut down.

8

Financial planning

Financial planning, along with the marketing plan, occupies a central position among the component parts of company planning.

The various strategies and alternatives are evaluated in the financial plan in respect of their profitability and the possibility of financing them. Thus the planning of the business culminates in the financial plan which forms the decisive test for all other areas. Financial planning has the following tasks:

- Checking the individual plans for their profitability, in order to secure the desired overall return for the business as a whole.
- Ensuring the liquidity of the firm.
- Making the best use of the cashflow.
- Covering the requirement for new capital.

As is evident from these tasks, financial planning does not consist of projecting the firm's bookkeeping and accounts into the future, but evaluating alternatives and planning new activities.

Planning the return

The achievement of a suitable return on capital invested is an important objective of every activity of the firm. If an acceptable long-term return cannot be achieved, it is better to liquidate the firm and invest the capital elsewhere.

Establishing what is the current rate of return on capital invested in the firm is the starting point for planning. Balance sheet figures should not be used for this purpose. Older firms, especially, may have hidden reserves which are often overlooked in calculating the returns. They often have hidden reserves in the form of land which may stand in the books at a conventional figure that can easily be one-twentieth or even one-hundredth of its market value. Houses and other real estate belonging to the firm usually appear in the accounts at a fraction of their market value. The firm's return on capital should be calculated on the basis of the market value of the firm and of all its assets, since it is to be expected that voluntary liquidation, not carried out under pressure of time, would release capital to this value which could be invested elsewhere.

A well-known petrol company owned a network of petrol stations, many of them in urban areas. Because of the growth of towns and the increase in land prices, the ground on which the pumps were standing had become so valuable that the profits from selling petrol had no relation to the value of the plots. In consequence, many of the petrol stations were closed and the plots were either sold or used for building office blocks. Some of the money was used for building or renting petrol stations in favourable, but much cheaper locations on the outskirts of the cities and on main roads.

There are many firms that are making poor use of their assets and are consequently worth more dead than alive. One of the important tasks of planning the return on capital is to cause an adequate return to be earned by making full use of hidden reserves. It is not at all unusual for a profitable firm to be earning only 3 per cent on capital, taking into account the market value of all its hidden reserves, and for the owners to be quite unaware of this fact because they have calculated their returns on the basis of a balance sheet compiled for tax purposes.

A return on capital of 3 per cent after tax is too low to make all the trouble, work and risk of operating the company worth while, when first-class securities, such as shares, convertible bonds or bonds of leading firms in the chemical or electrical industries can offer a return of 5 per cent to 8 per cent.

The return from the activity of the firm should therefore be considerably higher than these values. If the company appraisal reveals that an appropriate return is not being achieved, the improvement of the return must be a central point in the company objectives. This can often be brought about by separating unused or insufficiently used assets, such as land, and realising them. Tax regulations and tax loopholes must be carefully considered in any of these financial operations to avoid excessive tax payments caused by stripping. But it only makes sense to sell hidden reserves to finance expansion if the potential expansion of the firm is sufficiently profitable.

Cashflow planning

Long-term planning must be concerned with the question of the application of money derived from depreciation and retained profits. It is important to decide as early as possible whether to use this money within the existing activities of the firm, for example, for investment in rationalisation and the extension of facilities, or whether to use it in new areas. Early cashflow planning is often the precondition for diversification. In this way, the danger of destroying capital can be avoided.

The case of the Westphalian cement industry is an example. New manufacturing processes resulted in sharply-reduced manufacturing costs, but also in the creation of surplus capacity. Over investment caused cement prices to fall rapidly from £7 to £3 per ton. Only a few firms recognised the trend of events early enough and used their cashflow, not for extending their cement plants, but for diversifying into other building materials, such as lightweight building materials or ready-mix concrete, or for lateral diversification measures. By this means, they were able to take out at least part of the capital tied up in their cement plants.

Many medium-sized firms had no forward-looking planning: they went on ploughing money back into cement plant until powerful competition from the large firms, together with the price collapse, forced them to give up the struggle. The plants had to be sold for scrap. The capital invested, much of it only partly depreciated, was lost and could not be used for financing diversification projects.

Liquidity planning

Liquidity planning is usually a matter of short-term planning within the accounting framework, but in long-term planning periods of shortage of liquid resources can sometimes be foreseen. Thus, it is one of the tasks of company planning to check whether and, if so, when shortages are likely to occur and to take measures to circumvent them.

Shortage of cash is a frequent cause of collapse in firms. Even if it does not lead to catastrophe, it can force the company to abandon partially completed projects under unfavourable conditions. The fruits of years of hard work can be lost. Shortage of resources is the more dangerous the later it is detected. Hence, long-term planning must help to avoid it.

Cash management

A very effective way of reducing the need for liquid resources by better organisation is to institute cash management.

As part of cash management, the workflow in the sales accounting section may be speeded up so that invoices reach the customers as quickly as possible. Meeting the creditors' accounts is also carried out according to a time plan, making the best use of discounts, but not gratuitously making a present of the suppliers' period of credit.

The second important element in cash management is careful supervision and coordination of all bank accounts and the liquid assets of the firm, and managing them according to a precise timetable.

In order to have a sufficient safety margin, credit lines are agreed with the company's bankers, which are only to be used in case of need and then at the most favourable interest terms, according to the length of time for which it will be needed and the current situation in the money market.

Large firms will find that it pays to employ a cash manager whose job is to keep the firm's liquid resources turning over as quickly as possible, and to make

Planning the capital requirement 81

precise arrangements for the optimum handling of creditors' and debtors' accounts.

Analysis of the accounts of American firms shows that they have been able to support sharp increases in turnover with little or no increase in liquid resources, through skilful cash management. This not only reduces their need for capital, but also considerably increases their profitability by reducing the cost of servicing the capital.

Further means of **improving the liquidity** of the firm without taking up short or long time capital (claiming credit from suppliers, taking out loans or admitting new partners) are:

- Leasing instead of buying machines and facilities (e.g. buildings, machine tools, fork lift trucks, etc).
- Doing without support services, such as building units, transport fleets, data processing units, and using other firms and suppliers.
- Delaying new purchases and major maintenance works.
- Control of stocks and debtors.

These are essentially long-term measures for influencing the liquidity of the firm that have to be prepared well in advance. Thus, they are a proper part of company planning.

Planning the capital requirement

In order to plan the necessary measures for covering the **future need for capital,** the timing and size of that need have to be established. The following factors must be taken into account:

- Cashflow from future profits and depreciation.
- Payments to partners and shareholders.
- Capital requirements for existing activities (product development, **expansion** of sales organisation).
- Capital requirements for new activities (diversification).
- Available capital.
- Shortfall of capital.

Capital requirements in existing markets

In establishing the future need for capital in existing markets, the following points must be checked:

- Investment required (for design development and extension of production facilities).
- Capital needed for intensification of sales and for building up distribution and warehousing at home and abroad.
- Working capital needed for increasing production, inventory and sales.

- Rationalisation that will be needed to protect the firm's position in the market, as affected by technical developments, the competitive situation or government intervention.

Since 1965 the fertiliser industry has been installing large production units with an output of 2000 tons per day and operating costs of £2 per ton. Previously units with a daily output of 500 tons and operating costs of £3 per ton were usual. Firms that wished to stay in the fertiliser industry had no choice but to 'retreat forwards' into new super-installations at very considerable capital cost.

In the air transport industry heavy investment has been forced upon firms by technical developments. The supercession of the propeller by jets at the end of the 1950s, the introduction of jumbo jets, and, from 1974 onwards, of supersonic aircraft, are examples of 'forced' investment on the part of the airlines which sometimes drove them to the limit of their capital capability and significantly affected profits through high running-in costs and high depreciation. But firms often only have the choice between investing and leaving the industry, because the competitor has the higher capacity machines and is in too strong a competitive position. Similar developments are to be expected in the future in many branches of building materials and chemicals: new production processes mean lower unit costs, but larger plants. Such technical developments must be studied very carefully because they frequently lead to excess capacity and a price collapse in the whole industry.

Changes in the production of washing powders and detergents to meet new government requirements involved the manufacturers in substantial costs. In future we may expect similar problems because of more stringent control of air and water pollution. In the 1970s, paper mills, oil refineries, steel works, tanneries and dyeworks will be the victims of substantial involuntary investment.

Capital requirements for new products

When establishing the capital requirements for new areas of activity the following factors must be taken into account:

- The development of new products, not merely to the prototype stage, but to the stage of being fully marketable, including the necessary tests and market investigations. Experience shows that development engineers and technologists nearly always underestimate these costs. They often regard the development work as completed with the construction of the prototype. But considerable costs can still be incurred before the product becomes fully suitable for manufacture and for the market, especially in markets characterised by severe competition and sophisticated technology.
- Investment for production, distribution and sales facilities or for buying other firms.

- Working capital, including semifinished stocks in production and finished stocks in distribution and sales.
- Running-in costs until the breakeven point is reached, sometimes including heavy introductory advertising.

Mobilisation of capital reserves

When establishing the extent of the existing capital resources, hidden reserves such as undervalued properties deserve special attention. The same holds for manufacturing plant or sections of the product line which will not be needed in future or which are to be run down. By selling them early, as going sections of the firm, considerable sums of money can often be mobilised. Brand rights and licences for the same products offer similar possibilities of raising cash.

In 1969, the owner of the Melitta-Werke handled the closure of his subsidiary, a biscuit firm named Feurich Kekse in Munich, very skilfully. He had bought the firm in 1960, but realised soon afterwards that the opportunities for making a profit in the biscuit market were of little interest, because of strong competition, excess capacity and depressed prices.

He sold the machinery and the brand names to Bahlsen AG of Hanover, another biscuit manufacturer, and sold the factory site to Siemens, the large electrical firm, who needed it urgently to expand their neighbouring factory. Through this transaction, Herr Bentz received a considerably higher total price than he would have been able to get for a complete biscuit factory in the then depressed state of the market.

Establishing priorities

If it turns out that after exploiting all possible reserves it is still impossible to provide the capital needed for satisfying future demands in existing and in new areas of activity, the question of priorities arises. Which projects are to be implemented, and which given up? This question can only be answered with reference to the company objectives. If higher turnover and profits are the main objective, then the projects with the weakest prospects of turnover and profits are the losers. It should not, however, be overlooked that turnover and profit forecasts in new markets do not have the same degree of reliability as those in existing markets. The technique of risk-analysis can be used, to present the relative probability of the expected profits. If, however, the main company objective is diversification in order to reduce dependence on existing markets, it would be reasonable to give preference to projects in new markets, provided always that the prospect of a satisfactory profit has been confirmed by careful market investigation and calculation of the return.

The decision to finance new plans at the cost of projects in existing areas, or even the liquidation or sale of sections of the firm in favour of new projects with a better, but as yet uncertain future, remains a question of entrepreneurial daring.

The entrepreneur Willi Kaus, owner of the Metzeler company, showed this kind of courage when he decided to let Bayer have a 50 per cent share in his firm of Wolff Plastics. He needed the money for investment in Metzeler to put its finances on a sound footing prior to further expansion. In the next fifteen years he succeeded in building up the rundown firm of Metzeler from 3500 employees and £12 million turnover to 23 000 employees and £100 million turnover.

The Lübeck entrepreneur Alfred Hagelstein decided similarly to give up a sound operation in order to finance new entrepreneurial risks. In November 1969, he sold the hydraulic excavator section of his firm Hatra to Rheinstahl. He had developed this product line from nothing between 1964 and 1969 and had reached a turnover of £4 million. Rheinstahl paid a good price because it was suffering from poor profits in coal and steel and was very concerned to achieve a higher added value for its products by processing them further in the machine construction industry.

Hagelstein had chosen his moment very skilfully. For many years, hydraulic excavators had been the domain of medium-sized engineering firms, such as Liebherr, Fuchs, Poclain, Hagelstein, and others. As the market increased in size, large firms began to get interested, such as Demag and the American Koehring group. The era of market saturation, excess capacity and falling prices was threateningly near.

Hagelstein's intention was to invest his *rheinstahlgold* in the leisure market. He erected a large holiday centre on the Baltic coast with a marina, hotels, etc. This is an area of activity with great prospects for the future and no danger of competition from large firms.

Share marketing: the key to expansion

If the available capital is still not enough to finance profitable objectives when all the reserves have been mobilised and the scope for taking out loans has been exhausted, the only way out is to take on new equity capital. As the amount of available loan capital is usually limited to a certain proportion of the firm's own capital, the creation of new equity capital is an important way of financing ambitious objectives. An essential consideration for the entrepreneur is to buy the capital cheaply in relation to the prospective profits: to get as much equity capital as possible for every £1 of profit. The P/E ratio for the new capital should be as high as possible.

If the stock exchange investors are willing to pay a high P/E ratio, then the issue of shares can be a cheap source of new long-term capital for the firm.

The considerations that lead to the acquisition of capital on favourable terms are the same, whatever the legal status of the company, but it is generally easier for a public company to raise new equity capital. In financial planning, the

Share marketing: the key to expansion

question must be considered whether the company objectives are sufficiently important to justify a change in legal status in order to facilitate the provision of the capital needed to implement the objectives.

The department store owner Helmut Horten chose this solution. He turned his firm, which had a turnover of about £200 million in 1969 into a public company and sold 50 per cent of the shares on the market, in order to pay off loan capital and create a sounder financial structure for the company as a basis for further expansion. By only selling 50 per cent of the shares he protected himself against the possibility of losing control of his company to large outside shareholders.

The shares were sold at a P/E ratio of 14 and brought in more than £50 million. That means that for every £1 of expected company profit the new shareholders paid £14, or, calculated the other way round, for every £100 of capital provided by the new shareholders, Horten has to earn £7·15 in overall profit, including money retained in the company for hidden reserves and similar legally concealed features of profit and loss accounting. Only a part of this amount, between £3·50 and £4·50 need be actually paid out as dividends if Horten follows the dividend policy that is customary among German department store companies.

A loan would have involved annual interest payment of about £8·50 for every £100 borrowed – and that independently of whether the firm operates successfully or whether the competition from discount stores brings lean years in the future for Horten. This example shows how shareholders' money can be very cheap money, if they are prepared to pay a high P/E ratio for the shares. Thus share marketing is an important condition for financing expansion on favourable terms.

The stock exchange is willing to pay a premium for strong growth. The key word 'growth' means that the investing public is willing to pay a higher than average P/E ratio for the shares of the firm in question.

An expansion-conscious firm therefore has the task of acquiring the reputation of having growth prospects with the object of:

- Preparing the market for the issue of new shares (cultivating the market);
- Motivating the investing public to pay a price with a higher than average P/E ratio for the new shares.

The objective of share marketing is therefore to win the confidence of the investing public and to sell the idea of **the firm as a growth prospect.** To be successful, it requires reliable answers to the following questions:

- Who are the current and the potential purchasers of my shares? That is, private investors, banks, funds, insurance companies.
- What is their current view of my company and its shares?
- Who are the most important opinion-forming persons and institutions, towards whom information about my firm should be directed?

- What methods of giving information and promoting sales are the most appropriate?
- What circles or people must be contacted and how can this best be done?

In principle, the same considerations apply as for market planning in commerce and capital goods. But the methods of share marketing are considerably more difficult and more refined.

Shareholders' money is cheaper when the stock market is high

European firms have hitherto been much less successful than their American competitors in cultivating and extending their share markets.

While American firms can achieve a P/E ratio of 35, few European public companies achieve more than 16. Even the leaders in the German electrical, automobile and chemical industries whose results compare favourably with those of their American competitors and whose future prospects are extraordinarily good have far lower P/E ratios than their American counterparts.

SELECTED P/E RATIOS OF LEADING FIRMS (MID 1969)			
Bayer	12	Eastman Kodak	31
AEG	16	General Electric	22
Siemens	14	Honeywell	35
VW	8	General Motors	14

The Americans have evidently learned how to get better prices for their share capital. They can get more dollars from the public for each dollar of profit, if they finance investments or purchases of firms by issuing shares at the market price. Their own capital is therefore cheaper. The reason is that skilful cultivation of the Stock Exchange is regarded as an important task of their top management, while short-sighted dividend policies often restrict the growth of European share prices. Many European boards prefer to finance their firms as far as possible out of earnings and retain the lion's share of the profit as reserves, even though the taxman gets half of it. The argument is that the firm must equip itself for its future tasks. This is often a dubious policy: if the firm were kinder to its shareholders over the distribution of profits, the P/E ratio would be improved. Further tasks could then be financed more cheaply by issuing new shares at the market price.

Cultivating the market: a task for the board

In other ways than this, European firms do not take enough trouble about improving their standing on the Stock Exchange. In the USA share marketing is a major job. As a rule, one member of the board is specially responsible for relations with Wall Street, and he regards it as highly important to talk to the influential financial analysts who advise the brokers and investment funds. His job is to 'sell' his firm and thus to create the conditions for financing its further growth.

In the USA it is regarded as a good sign and as something to be pleased and proud about if the price of the firm's shares rises. Not so with European managements: the share price is taboo. They often even try to neutralise the effect of increases in turnover and good results by gloomy remarks about the dark future, heavy demands and risks of the next few years, uncertain economic conditions, and so on. They try to conceal good results from the shareholders by appropriate manipulation of the published accounts, for fear of provoking gluttonous demands for dividends. If increased dividends are 'unavoidable' they are sometimes camouflaged as bonuses.

They fail to see that the shareholder is management's most important partner in the cultivation of the share price.

Publicity – a burden?

In their annual reports and at the shareholders' meetings, the Americans discuss not only their successes in increasing turnover and profits, but also their detailed plans for the future. They know that the Stock Exchange will often pay more for future hopes than for present and past figures. The result is that even in the European economic Press one reads about projects for the future, such as electric motor-cars, fuel cells, plastic houses, turbine-driven trucks, and so on, taken from the reports of American firms. Specialists are well aware that European firms have been working on such projects for years. But European firms are shy of publicity. They give way to their research departments' congenital secret-mongering even over decisive questions of the firm's publicity.

This is not only stupid, but unrealistic. What is going on in the firm's research laboratories is usually well known to the specialists in the competitive firms. To withhold it from the shareholders or potential shareholders harms nobody except the firm itself. To sell shares at a favourable price, a firm must first sell its own future.

Share options for executives

American firms take trouble to commit their managements to the growth of their firm's share prices. Stock options for executives are common. They give the right to buy shares at a stated future time (e.g. three years after joining the company) at the price at which the shares stood when the manager joined the company.

If share prices rise, these options are worth a lot of money. If they do not rise, or even fall, they are worth nothing. Stock options are a good incentive to managers to achieve a high performance and to let the shareholders participate in the success of the firm in the form of higher dividends and higher share prices. That also means that there is little interest in unnecessarily high reserves.

9

The strategy of conglomerates

Conglomerates are firms whose business policy is not based on the skill or knowledge of the firm in particular product or market areas, but whose objectives are to achieve the highest possible return on capital by buying firms in any branch of industry. As already stated, P/E ratios of 20 and higher for the purchase of successful firms are not uncommon. This figure shows that expansion by means of acquisitions can only be financially successful if suitable sources of finance are accessible. Bank credits and loans are not suitable for financing continued expansion by takeovers. The use of cash for this purpose also leads to a sharp fall in the firm's return on capital.

Conglomerates therefore make use of share marketing to create the financial conditions for their expansion policies. Financing by exchange of shares or by issuing new shares permits them to buy firms at high P/E ratios without watering down their own return on capital. The necessary condition is that the price of the firm's own shares represents a higher P/E ratio than the price of the firm that is being taken over.

The following example will clarify this principle. The firms of Smith Ltd and Jones Ltd are both trying to buy Robinson Ltd. The owners of Robinson are asking a price that corresponds to a P/E ratio of 20 and would accept an exchange of shares. The price of Smith shares on the Stock Exchange corresponds to a P/E ratio of 30, but Jones's shares stand at only 12. The table on the next page shows what the position would be in both firms, before and after taking over Robinson.

Success breeds success. The firm with a high P/E ratio can afford to buy other firms. The shareholders benefit from a higher profit per share and a higher share price. The firm with a low P/E loses out. Profit per share and share price fall.

Smith could raise their profit per share from £2 to £2·14 by the amalgamation, in spite of issuing new shares to finance the takeover. Jones's profit per share would drop from £2 to £1·77, and their shareholders would be threatened by a fall in share prices if the company's results still give a P/E ratio of 12:1.

89

The significance of the P/E ratio for the decision to purchase a firm

Before the purchase

	SMITH LTD	JONES LTD
Number of shares	10 000 000	10 000 000
Nominal value per share	£1	£1
Share capital	£10 000 000	£10 000 000
Profit after tax	£2 000 000	£2 000 000
Profit per share	£0·2	£0·2
P/E ratio	30	12
Market price of shares	£6	£2·4

ROBINSON LTD
Profit after tax   £500 000
Purchase price   £10 000 000 in shares (= 20 × profit)
                = 1 670 000 new Smith shares
                or 4 160 000 new Jones shares

After the purchase

	SMITH LTD	JONES LTD
Number of shares	11 670 000	14 160 000
Profit	£2 500 000	£2 500 000
Profit per share	£0·214	£0·177
P/E ratio	30	12
Market price of shares	£6·42	£2·124

Although the profit per share is not so easy to elicit for European firms as for American firms because of differing accounting procedures, the P/E ratio is coming to be used as an important criterion in the European stock exchanges.

The table shows that because the P/E ratio, the profit per share and the growth in profit per share are three of the most important criteria for fixing the price of shares, takeovers can in general only be initiated by firms that have a higher than average P/E ratio for their shares on the Stock Exchange.

That is why conglomerates have to make sure that their shares always have a higher than average price on the stock market. So long as the market is highly growth conscious, this can be achieved by skilful public relations and share marketing. If a conglomerate can acquire the reputation of being a growth stock, the investing public is willing to pay at a higher than normal P/E ratio for its shares.

This was especially true in the USA prior to 1968 as is shown by a comparison of the P/E ratios of American conglomerates.

It is evident, therefore, that the strategy of conglomerates is based on the psychological attitude of the investing public, and especially of investment

The strategy of conglomerates

funds, to growth. Growth is measured in profit per share, and people are willing to pay for it in the form of a high P/E ratio. A P/E ratio of 20 means that the market is willing to pay £20 for a share with a profit after tax of £1 per share.

For so long as the conglomerate succeeds in buying firms with a lower P/E ratio than its own shares, its own profit per share keeps on rising. This even happens if the profit is not improved by any integration effect. The increase in profit per share through buying existing firms still comes about, even if there is no improvement in the parent firm's profitability by rationalisation of production or improvement of sales.

It is enough for the profit per share to rise as a result of the effect of the takeover on the parent firm's accounts. For the Stock Exchange this is proof of successgrowth. This, in turn, confirms the investors' view that the previous high P/E ratio was indeed justified.

The whole thing is a snowball system. If the profit per share goes on rising through continuous takeovers, the high P/E ratio stands. But if the profit per share falls because of unexpected setbacks, the conglomerate loses its halo of being a growth stock and the P/E ratio falls. This means that the conditions for increasing profits by further takeovers have vanished. The conglomerate then has to get down to the hard task of raising profits by better performance of the parent company. Experience shows that this brings the managers of conglomerates a great deal less joy than making takeovers.

Since 1968, there has been a fundamental change in the market climate for conglomerates. The investors on the stock markets recognised that the technical effects of takeovers on the conglomerates' accounts did not represent genuine growth and were no longer prepared to pay excessive P/E ratios for their shares. A number of conglomerates also suffered from unexpected setbacks in their real profits. They lost the reputation of growth stocks and their share prices and P/E ratios fell rapidly. The efforts of the US antitrust authorities to prevent excessive concentration of the American economy also had an important effect.

The following are the P/E ratios of some leading American conglomerates in 1968 and 1969. The fall in their share prices to very low levels provides evidence that the snowball effect of takeovers has been interrupted. Whether the conglomerates' strategy of achieving rapid growth by acquisitions and associated financial manoeuvres is a thing of the past remains to be seen.

	P/E ratio	
	1968 High	1969 Low
Gulf & Western Industries	21	5
ITT	24	12
Litton Industries	56	8
Textron	28	10

10

Product planning

The purpose of product planning is to develop the products that the company needs in order to reach its market objectives. It may be a matter of developing new products or of improving or adapting existing ones.

From the point of view of company planning, it does not matter whether realisation of the product plan involves research and development or only styling or design. Similarly, product planning is concerned both with products for existing markets and for diversification, in so far as the latter are not acquired by purchasing another firm.

The idea that a new product and therewith a profitable position in the market will fall into the company's lap like an overripe plum through a creative act of genius, does not form a realistic basis for well-directed product development.

It is decisive for the success of an enterprise that the scope and direction of product development shall be determined by the company's objectives and potential in the market. Product planning therefore starts with the **questions**:

- What demands will the market make on the company's products in the future?
- What will have to be done in research, development and manufacture to meet these demands?

The market is the dominating influence, even over the technical problems of applied research and development. Market planning decides in which markets the firm will be active in the future. Product planning ensures that the products needed in these markets are developed and manufactured.

This order of priorities is fundamental. It often happens that the technologists develop and produce products first and only when they have been made does the firm begin to think about how to sell them. When sellers' markets were the rule in most branches of industry, this procedure was practicable. Nowadays with increasing competition and 'spoilt' customers, this procedure entails the danger that high costs in money and time are incurred for research, development and manufacture of products that do not offer sufficient market opportunities for profitable sales.

Priorities for development proposals

Every firm, even a giant like Lockheed or Rolls-Royce, has limited resources at its disposal for development and design, because of shortages of personnel, time and money. Hence, it is important to apply these resources in a well-decided manner with the best prospects of future success in the market. This objective can only be achieved if technical planning is integrated into company planning. This does not mean that the company planners are responsible in practice for development and design. But project proposals from these departments must be checked from the point of view of company planning. Product development is much too important for the firm to be left to the specialists in research and development.

In order to ensure agreement between market planning and technical product development, those areas must first be selected out of the vast possibilities of technical and scientific development which offer realistic opportunities for marketing the results of successful development work. The firm's activities in applied research and development are then concentrated in these areas. Regular and critical review is extremely important. Every firm is in the situation of having plenty of projects that might be developed, only a fraction of which can actually be carried out within the research and development capacity of the firm and within the cost limits set by considerations of profitability and liquidity.

Product planning has to decide on orders of **priority** between development proposals by answering the following questions:

- Can the product that is expected as the successful outcome of a development process be sold successfully?
- What is the relation of the likely cost of development up to the point of putting the product on the market, to the market potential?

In order to prevent development costs from being wasted on marginal or unprofitable projects, it is strongly recommended that projects should be critically examined before development work starts.

In addition, projects should be submitted to reexamination during the development work at least annually, if not more often. This should be coupled with the authorisation for further expenditure, since research and development departments must not be allowed to spend money at will, but must work within the framework of annual expenditure budgets subdivided by projects. This is an important condition for integrating the technical area into the overall company planning. Budgets for individual projects are only released after they have been authorised by product planning.

It is absolutely necessary to reexamine development projects at least annually for the following reasons:

- The original grounds on which the decision to develop the product was taken nearly always have to be revised during the development work. Thus, it may happen that the product can now be expected to have more favourable characteristics than was originally supposed; or unexpected technical difficulties may have arisen, which will substantially increase the costs that will be incurred before the product is ready to go on the market.
- The market situation may have changed because of new competitors or technical developments. Thus, the German coal industry carried out an expensive development effort on the gasification of coal in order to supplement the supplies of coke-oven gas, which were running short, and to increase the demand for coal. All this work became pointless when cheap natural gas became available in North Germany and Holland. But the project was only dropped many years after its justification had disappeared.

To ensure a rational control of technical development it must be remembered that the costs incurred in the early stages of development are usually low, and then grow progressively as the work comes up to the stage of market readiness. The later the decision to close a project is taken, the higher are the wasted development costs, and an abandoned development project can have an injurious effect on the firm's market position in other areas, through occupying the time of personnel that might have been used on other projects with better chances of success. The time lost on unprofitable projects can often do more harm to the company than the wasted costs.

Regular critical examination as early as possible helps to avoid this danger.

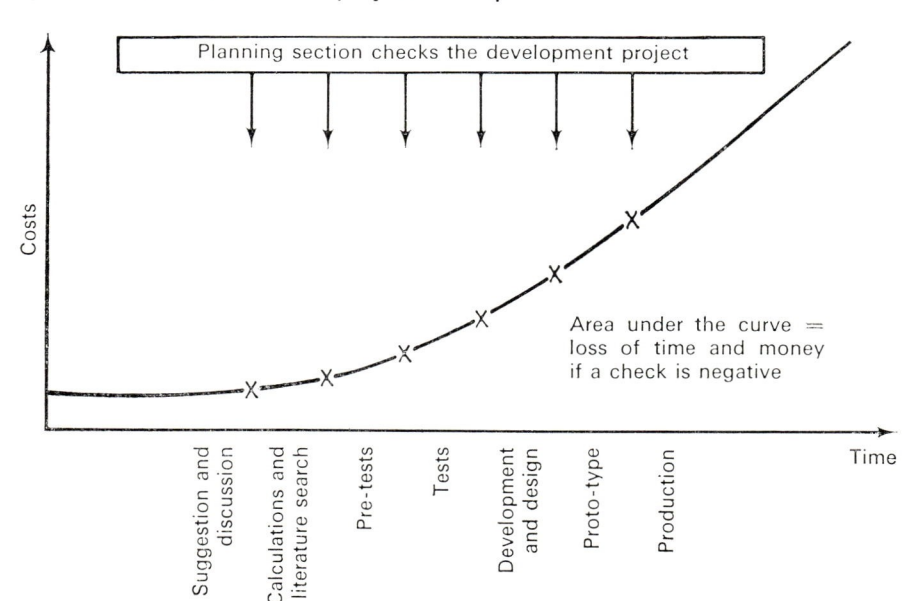

Fig. 10.1 Time lost curve for project development

Priorities for development proposals

The overriding importance of integrating technical development into company planning can be shown from the attempts, which up to now have been unsuccessful, to develop new kinds of internal combustion engine and put them on the market. NSU invested substantial resources in the development of the Wankel motor between 1955 and 1967, estimated at more than £4 million. This was too much of a drain on the firm's resources since NSU was the smallest of the German manufacturers of passenger cars and had a turnover of less than £50 million in 1967. Up to the time of its amalgamation with VW Auto-Union, the firm achieved no significant sales or licensing arrangements for its Wankel project. In 1968, 6000 cars with Wankel engines were produced. The Chairman of NSU, who was the father of the Wankel project, said in 1970 'The last obstacle for the Wankel motor is servicing. The car manufacturers do not believe that the service garages can be expected to carry out the considerable new tasks that will arise out of the introduction of this engine.'

An American industrialist and inventor called Lear worked on the development of a steam-engine for motor-cars from 1964 to 1969. Its particular advantage was that it would solve the problem of exhaust gases in American cities. After he had invested nearly £3 million in the project he gave up.

'Even if we solve the technical problems, servicing the steam-engine will be so difficult that it will not be able to compete with the conventional petrol engine in the eyes of car-owners.'

In both cases, the technical advantages of the new engines were overestimated and the importance of other factors that influence sales were underestimated. The new products were entering into competition with the seventy-five-year-old piston engine, which is highly developed not only technically and as regards cost, but also in respect of ease of servicing, and they were doing this in the highly developed automobile market.

The car owner is concerned about the roominess and styling of his car, its interior finish and the size of the boot, its roadholding, acceleration and braking. He is only interested in what is under the bonnet in so far as it works and can be readily serviced. Technical details of the engine have virtually no influence on the decision to buy a particular make. These facts, which are obvious to the marketing man, were apparently regarded by the 'fathers' of the Wankel engine and the steam-engine as much less important than the hoped-for technical advantages and the attractions of novelty.

Mr Lear was able to withstand the temptation to go on tinkering and cut the project off after a cool appraisal of its chances of success.

NSU no longer exists as an independent firm, having been acquired by VW. If the development work on the Wankel motor should after all lead to success at some future date, VW will get the benefit. It is possible that the money that was invested in the Wankel project could have been put to better use within the framework of NSU company planning.

There are other firms that have been spending money for decades on developing new motors. In the 1930s, Philips NV of Holland took up the idea of the Stirling hot-air engine, invented a century earlier by a Scottish parson called

Robert Stirling. It was originally intended to be used to generate electricity for radios on remote farms without electric supply, but the development of transistors made it possible to power radios with cheap batteries. Although reports continue to appear in the technical Press about development work on the Stirling engine, nothing significant has yet reached the market in spite of forty years of costly development work. Only after Philips experienced a severe profit-squeeze in 1971 was the Stirling Project curtailed.

Working out the product specification

Product planning can help considerably towards increasing the effectiveness and the chances of success in technical development. Technologists are inclined, as is well known, to see their job primarily as one solving technical problems, and are not market oriented. Product planning can play the role of interpreter and translate the demands of the market and the interests of market planning into the technologists' language. In so doing, product planning will define the **technical characteristics of a product** in such a way as to give it the best possible chance of success on the market. The following questions have to be answered:

- In which segments of the market is the product most likely to sell well?
- What should the product be like, to give it the best chance of selling?
- For what features of the product is the customer willing to pay more or to change brand?
- What properties make the product more expensive without increasing its usefulness to the customer?

In order to develop a new kind of internal combustion engine in a well-directed manner, with the best prospects of success, product planning would first have to decide what would be the most promising applications of the engine. Applications that might be considered are:

Passenger cars;
Engines for light aircraft;
Drive for lawnmowers;
Drive for electric generators;
Engines for small boats;
Drive for fire-fighting pumps.

Not only is the size of these different market segments very different in terms of units to be sold, but the technical and economic demands are very different for each application. Thus, the prospects of penetrating them and replacing the piston engine vary widely in each case.

Product planning would have to investigate very carefully in each segment of the market what were the demands, the influences on the decision to buy, the

Working out the product specification

competitive situation and the selling conditions, in order to establish the optimal market for the new engine. It would then define the technical and economic properties that the engine would be required to possess, in order to be successful.

As a drive for electric generators, the demand for low weight, high reliability and long life would be important. As a drive for lawnmowers, cheapness and low noise output would matter most.

On the basis of considerations of this kind, product planning can set up specifications which give research workers and designers a target to work towards, and thus substantially increase their chance of success.

Product planning is not only the controller, who shoots down the technologists' projects, but is also the pathfinder of technical development, who makes the work of the technical people a great deal easier and increases their chances of success.

Checklist 8 Product planning

1 How large is the market for the new product and how is it expected to develop in the future?

2 Who are the competitors?

3 What are the characteristics of the competitors' products?

4 Are the customers currently satisfied with the technical characteristics of the available products?

5 In what direction are the customers' technical demands expected to change?

6 Does the company have proper facilities for selling the product? Can a suitable sales organisation and customer service be built up?

7 What share of the market can the company expect to capture? Is this enough for economical production?

8 By what date at the latest must the new product be available, if the sales targets are to be achieved?

9 What technical and economic characteristics must the product have in order to penetrate the market and to persuade customers to change from the makes they are buying at present? What are the required features of:

> performance, length of useful life, shape, style, colour, reliability, purchase price, operating costs, spares, customer service.

10 What is the relative importance of these features in the customers' eyes? What features determine the decision to buy?

11 For what properties are the customers willing to pay a higher price?

12 At what price is the product acceptable to the market?

11

Weakness of futurology and market research for company planning

Company planning is concerned with future market conditions and the capacity of the firm to maintain its position in future markets successfully. Futurology is also concerned with questions of future developments. It is most concerned, however, with sociological questions: future changes in value judgments, in community living, urban planning, and so on. In so far as futurologists make pronouncements about future economic developments, these are mostly of a very general character, e.g.:

- Underwater exploration will be very important.
- The production of agricultural products in underdeveloped countries will have to be increased if famine and revolution are to be avoided.
- Motor vehicles will be driven by new kinds of engine, to avoid air pollution.
- Three-dimensional TV will come.
- Data processing over telephone lines will be used not only in offices and factories, but also in the home.

Such pronouncements are too non-committal and vague to give the company planner anything to build on. An engineering firm that is wondering whether to manufacture diving equipment for underwater exploration needs answers to certain detailed questions, namely:

- How big is the market now?
- How fast will it grow in the next five years?
- How is the demand divided between military, government and industrial users?
- What technical demands (size, diving depth, etc) are to be expected?

The firm's company planner will not get answers to these questions from the futurologists. Even when futurology is done seriously (in the opinion of the author it seldom is), influential authors and speakers confine themselves to non-committal utopian descriptions of the distant future, combined with hair-raising warnings of atomic doom. What they say about the volume and timing of the new markets is far too vague to be any use to a rational company planner.

In appraising these forecasts, it is also to be noted that the public interest in futurological pronouncements is often skilfully exploited for advertising purposes. The car of the year 2000 with a rocket-like body, fuel cells, ejector seat and electronic controls is an object of admiration at every motor show. Press and TV reporters crowd in to file their reports. The advertising effectiveness of this reporting is so valuable for the exhibitors that the modest cost of building the model is one of the most effective elements in their advertising budget.

The submarines sponsored by large American firms that have been so enthusiastically reported in economic and technical journals have produced no financial returns for their constructors, but have brought a high public relations value to the surface.

Thus, it is the advertising people who have hitherto drawn more benefit from futurology than company planners. The author sees no likelihood that this situation will change. The year 2000, beloved of the futurologists, is too far ahead to give the company planner any leads for practical planning.

Market research as an aid to decisions

When appraising new markets the following are the main questions that are relevant to company planning:

- What new markets are suitable for a commitment on the part of my company?
- What is the sales potential of these markets?
- When will the potential be reached in practice? 1975, 1980, 2000?
- What will have to be done in development, production and sales to ensure an adequate market share for my firm?
- What will be the relation between sales and costs? Will it be possible for my firm to obtain an adequate return in this market?

Market research can elicit information that is useful for answering these points. In deciding between different market strategies or diversification proposals, company planning is particularly dependent on data that can only be provided by market research.

However, the market researcher who is working for the company planners must not forget that:

- Many of the data, such as the future growth rate of a new market, cannot be measured by any scientific method;
- A well-founded judgment is often just as important as calculated results arrived at by scientific methods.

Market researchers who are accustomed to deal mainly with market shares or media contact, and who therefore concentrate on technical problems in statistics, may have little competence over problems of company planning, since the likely sales in new markets cannot be estimated by formal methods alone.

Market research as an aid to decisions

Certain purely quantitative data are first required: how big is the market, how fast will it grow? This approach is familiar to market researchers, even though the future market volume can only be guessed at and not calculated.

But there are also qualitative considerations that are of decisive importance for company planning. Judgments have to be made about:

- The future demands of the customer, in their bearing on technology, economics, design, customer service and sales;
- The criteria that influence the consumer in his choice of brand;
- The firm's chances of penetrating the market.

The last question about possible market penetration can be clarified with the aid of the following information:

- Are the consumers aware of the advantages of the firm's products, or can they be made aware of them?
- Are the consumers satisfied with the competing products?
- Are the consumers ready to change brand in order to enjoy the advantages of the firm's product? Under what conditions?
- What demands of the consumer must the firm be able to satisfy in respect of sales and customer service?

These considerations show that the penetration possibilities of a Wankel engine, for example, or a fuel cell for motor-cars, do not depend primarily on the objective advantages of these products, but on whether the customers recognize the advantages and are willing to change from their present types and makes of car in order to enjoy the advantages of a vehicle powered by a Wankel engine. Experience shows that new inventions and developments often lead to disappointing results through underestimating this factor.

Appraising the firm's opportunities in new markets demands a multiplicity of information. In practice, it is seldom possible to come by all the desired information. There are many facts that cannot be arrived at with sufficient confidence. The number of users of long-distance data transmission equipment in 1980 can only be a guess. But this figure could be exceedingly important for a firm interested in the market for time-sharing EDP equipment.

The time and money available for every company planning decision is, in practice, limited. Market research must therefore be concentrated on the figures relevant to the decisions that are to be made at the time and the results worked out only to the degree of accuracy that is absolutely necessary. In investigating future markets, the cost in time and money of further work is often out of all proportion to the improvement in the accuracy and reliability of the results.

Experience shows that market researchers are strongly inclined to produce copious reports and tables that have no bearing on the problems facing the company planner. If market research is to be used successfully in company planning, it must be deliberately restricted to a small number of points that are really critical for the decisions that have to be made.

12

Manpower planning

The purpose of manpower planning is to ensure that the implementation of the company plan over the next five to seven years is not hindered by lack of suitable personnel. In addition, it should provide and encourage broadly based management development for employees with management potential.

In the next few years, the shortage of skilled labour in most European countries can only get worse. This is true of skilled workers, technical and management personnel. The causes lie in the unfavourable age structure of the population due to the war, and in the heavy demand due to rapid economic expansion.

Manpower planning is a long-term problem. The acquisition of business experience cannot be accelerated at will, and training measures are only effective over a considerable timespan.

Bringing in senior managers from outside under pressure of manpower shortage has serious drawbacks. It tends to increase the turnover of existing managers because they see their chances of promotion reduced. It also tends to disturb the level of salaries because good people usually have to be acquired at salaries above the market price.

The risk of mistakes is greater than is the case with internal promotions. It takes a year to discover whether the new man is up to the job, in spite of personnel consultants, handwriting analysts and psychoanalysts. If he is not good enough, a lot of time and money has been thrown away.

Manpower planning can therefore be a decisive factor in the implementation of company plans. Among its more important aspects are:

- Establishing the manpower position in terms of number, qualification and age.
- Appraising the promotion potential of employees, especially middle and senior managers and the next generation of managers.
- Estimating the future manpower needs, by number and qualifications, on the basis of the company plan and the future organisation structure.
- Planning what has to be done to meet future needs, such as recruitment, training, promotions and dismissals of staff.

Establishing the manpower position

It is not difficult to establish the current manpower position in quantitative terms (how many fitters, assembly workers, sales engineers, etc, are on the payroll; and how many will reach retiring age in the next five years). The personnel records should contain the required data.

The analysis should not be confined to present activities of individuals, but should include their education, qualifications, experience and potential. This will help the company to establish which individuals can be prepared for new jobs or for promotion by training, retraining or additional experience.

Regular appraisal by superiors

In order to obtain reliable information about employees' potential, it is desirable that the immediate superior should fill out an appraisal sheet once a year for all those under him, and should discuss it with his own superior and with the personnel officer. If this is done annually, it can be seen what progress the employee has made, what training courses he had attended, and whether he still has the potential for further promotion.

Although the appraisal is confined to a small number of characteristics at operator or weekly-paid level, it should still be carried out annually in order to provide the basis for future selection of skilled workers, chargehands, foremen and junior supervisors.

To confine the appraisal to middle and senior management would be to ignore an important reservoir of future managers at all levels. A regular appraisal procedure is a systematic way of identifying people with the proverbial field marshal's baton in their knapsacks. It also forms a way of deciding whether the firm can regenerate and expand out of its own manpower resources, or whether it will need blood transfusions from outside if it is to survive and grow.

Establishing the future need

The future manpower needs are first established on a quantitative basis. How many additional fitters, assembly workers, sales engineers, etc, shall we need in four years' time?

A purely quantitative approach is not, however, enough to establish the need for managers. It is important that the present and **future organisation structure** of the firm should be surveyed, in order to answer the following questions:

- Where in the hierarchy of the firm will it be necessary to create new managerial positions?
- Which of the existing positions are superfluous?
- Which positions will become empty as a result of retirement, transfers or resignations?
- Which positions are at present not filled satisfactorily?

The next step is to write job descriptions for all the future positions in the firm. The job descriptions should state the tasks and areas of responsibility of each position, and the required education, practical experience and age of the occupant. They form a useful aid not only in manpower planning, but also in the selection and recruitment of new personnel.

When establishing the **need for additional personnel,** the following factors must be taken into account:

- Increase in personnel needed by industrial sections, factories or subsidiaries;
- Future retirements;
- Dismissals of personnel whose performance is unsatisfactory;
- Losses through labour turnover.

Firms often underestimate the effect of labour turnover on manpower needs and, hence, on the capacity of training and recruitment programmes.

Turnover is calculated on the basis of employees who leave for reasons other than retirement or expansion or closure of sections of the firm. Apprentices and trainees are not included. The turnover rate is the ratio between the number of employees lost during the year and the total number of employees at the beginning of the year.

The turnover rate for hourly paid workers is usually about 15 to 25 per cent. For administrative staff, it is about 10 to 15 per cent and for middle and senior managers, about 10 to 20 per cent. Among sales representatives it is usually higher. In grocery sales, it is about 20 to 30 per cent.

There are, however, plenty of old-established firms in which the labour turnover is substantially lower, but experience shows that a low turnover rate is a warning signal. Perhaps the demands made on the employees are not very high. 'Nobody has ever been sacked here' is not necessarily a favourable reflection on the management of the firm.

The tables opposite show how to calculate the labour turnover rate, and how to estimate the manpower needs for a sales force. In this case, a furniture manufacturer needs to increase his sales force by twenty-five men over the next five years, i.e. from fifteen to forty between 1973 and 1978, in order to expand, to replace outside agents and to call directly on retail outlets. It shows that for each of the next five years he will need to recruit not five new representatives per year, but probably eleven to fifteen every year. The training and induction of this number of new personnel implies a considerable financial and operational burden for the firm.

Training and development of employees

Training and development is an area of manpower planning that will increase in importance in the future, both for hourly and weekly staff and for management. The reasons are:

- The firm's demands on the knowledge and skills of its employees are continuously rising. The traditional educational institutions (trade schools, technical colleges and universities) can only adjust slowly.

Example 3 Calculation of labour turnover

A	Employees at the beginning of the year (excluding apprentices and trainees)	900
B	Appointments due to expansion (existing or new employees)	60
C	Other appointments	230
D	Dismissals due to shortage of work, rationalisation or closures	10
E	Losses due to retirement	30
F	Other losses	200
G	Labour turnover $\left(\dfrac{F \times 100}{A + C}\right)$	17·7%

Example 4 Calculation of staff needed for the expansion of the sales force

		NUMBER OF REPRESENTATIVES					
		1973	'74	'75	'76	'77	'78
A	Planned staff size	15	20	25	30	35	40
B	Losses due to retirement	1	2	1	2	1	2
C	Subtotal	14	18	24	28	34	38
D	Turnover losses (estimated 20%)	3	4	5	6	7	8
E	Present staff	15					
F	Additional personnel needed for expansion	—	5	5	5	5	5
G	Recruitment required (B + D + F)	4	11	11	13	13	15

- The number of suitably trained workers and staff is inadequate. Firms used to be active only in the field of apprentice training. Today, the firm has to become an educator at all levels. But cost and benefit to the firm must be in a sensible relationship.

Training and development can only be properly directed towards the firm's needs if what it expects of its employees is clearly defined in the form of job descriptions.

Programmed learning texts have proved their value for training hourly and weekly employees. They are an effective solution to the problem of teaching the same relatively simple material to a large number of employees; for example, male and female assembly workers, salesmen, and technical sales and service staff.

The cost of developing a programmed learning text is high, but the use of the programme by large groups offers substantial advantages in the form of effectiveness and saving of time and money. If these conditions do not exist then traditional methods should be used, such as lectures, seminars and practical exercises.

Programmed learning has been used successfully by the firm of Klaus Esser, a well-known manufacturer of roof lights and other equipment for flat roofs. All the employees of this firm can learn about building techniques, processing synthetic materials and selling by means of programmed learning. The programmes were compiled with the assistance of an industrial sociologist. There is a final test, to show whether the participant has successfully assimilated the programme.

An additional advantage of making programmed learning available is that the principle of promotion through training is put into effect. The firm creates a broad basis for filling vacancies in production, sales and administration with qualified people drawn from its own employees.

Management development

The quality of managers is a significant competitive factor and the development of managers and of their successors is an important aspect of manpower planning. Most US firms spend a lot of time and money on management development.

Two complementary **methods of management development** are appropriate:
- Development through courses, lectures and seminars held inside and outside the firm.
- Rotation, i.e. putting a manager through a planned series of different jobs, for example, in purchasing, in the sales force, in sales management and accounts.

Development courses

There are many institutions in all European countries that offer seminars and lectures for managers, for example, in sales, accountancy, costing, personnel, and integrated courses for management development. A weakness of training through such institutions is that the courses are mostly very short (one to three days), with little coordination between the different courses in the same institution or between those of different institutions.

To avoid wasting time, it is recommended that for every employee for whom training is to be provided a training plan should be drawn up, so that his attendance at courses and seminars can be directed towards specific goals. It could be sensible, for example, for an assistant in a sales department who is being prepared for sales management, to attend a seminar one or two days each month over a period of one or two years on such subjects as principles of marketing, costing, advertising, sales indices, making a sale, market research, organisation of a sales force, control of representatives, sales budgets, route planning, etc.

Larger firms can organise their own seminars with advantage. This can be done in cooperation with a college or with a firm of management consultants. The advantage is that the courses can be tailored to the specific needs of the firm and the problems of its industry. Internal seminars can also serve the purpose of altering the basic attitudes of a whole group of employees. Certain engineering firms have equipped their technical and commercial managers with modern ideas about marketing by means of carefully planned in-firm courses. Mechanical engineers and electronics experts, mining engineers and lawyers whose ideas were stuck in technically-oriented grooves were introduced to market-oriented thinking.

Seminars conducted like school classes are not suitable for management training. Special techniques are required, that take account of the interests and inclinations as well as the aversions of the participants. Case studies are specially valuable, as they encourage creative participation in the solution of practical problems. They give the participants the opportunity to apply, at least in a simulated situation, the knowledge that they have gained in the seminar room and to make their own judgments about the scope and limitations of their newly acquired knowledge.

Rotation of managers

Job rotation is a well-tried method of broadening the knowledge and experience of managers. It is a good way of fighting specialisation and encouraging teamwork in the management of the firm. It is particularly well suited as preparation for senior executive positions, either as managing director of a subsidiary or on the board of the parent firm.

European firms have been hesitant about job rotation. How can one expect a purchasing manager to make a good sales manager, financial executive or production manager? This is where the basic difference between American and European attitudes to management shows up most clearly. The Americans emphasise that what is important for different management positions is not specialist knowledge of the subject, but knowledge and experience of management. Hence, a good purchasing manager can become a good sales manager, after a short period of induction. By this means, he gains insight and experience in different areas. The firm also gains the opportunity to judge how he shapes up to new problems.

Job rotation helps to make the work more interesting and varied. It works as a counter-influence to staff turnover. It also helps to improve understanding and cooperation between different sections of the firm.

The personnel manager: a new key position

The personnel manager has a key position in manpower planning. For firms of about 1000 employees upwards, a qualified personnel manager is essential for manpower planning. He should not, however, be a personnel administrator whose interests and activities are confined to wages and working conditions. He must be a manager capable of recognising and developing the potential of employees at all levels, if the crucial tasks of manpower planning and personnel development are to be carried out successfully. A checklist of his duties is given on the opposite page.

Checklist 9 The personnel manager's duties

1 Establish the future need for personnel by number and quality of employees on the basis of the manpower plan.
2 Procure job descriptions for all managerial positions.
3 Conduct appointment interviews, evaluate candidates. Make new appointments.
4 Develop and administer a wage and salary structure, including salary brackets for each position and incentive premiums.
5 Introduce and service a system of appraisal of all employees by their superior, as a basis for promotion and planning the filling of vacancies.
6 Identify employees suitable as successors to the present management.
7 Develop and administer internal and external training programmes, so that employees can become familiar with modern methods.
8 Work out individual training programmes (attendance at courses and seminars, job rotation) for managers and future managers worthy of promotion.
9 Administer all personnel records.
10 Organise and administer the social programmes (pension fund, life insurance, medical aid, canteen, sports club, etc).
11 Organise and administer suggestion schemes.
12 Represent the firm in matters relating to works council, trade unions, labour law, accident prevention.
13 Observe morale in the firm to take steps to keep it as high as possible.
14 Contact with employers' federations and employment officers at universities and colleges.

Limitation of responsibilities: The personnel manager is responsible for ensuring that the firm has at all times the right number and quality of employees. He cannot appoint, dismiss or promote anyone or award any increase in wages or salary without the consent of the functional manager concerned. He cannot make any alterations in the organisation structure of the firm without the consent of the manager concerned.

13

Organisation planning in the growing firm

The purpose of organisation planning is to arrange the tasks and responsibilities of the employees in such a way as to maximise the performance of the firm. In practice, this requires:

- Avoiding unnecessary overlapping of tasks and responsibilities of individual employees, especially managers;
- Defining and delimiting the responsibilities of managers clearly;
- Formulating objectives for individual managers, so that their performance can be measured by their implementation of the objectives. This requires a budgetary control system with regular comparison of budget and actual figures (e.g. sales figures, production costs, stock turnround, etc).

In a growing firm, the tasks are continually changing in nature, scope and importance, and the organisation must be continually adapted to the new circumstances. Bad organisation leads to losses through internal antagonisms, unnecessary costs and lack of flexibility. In the long term, poor organisation can damage a firm's growth and profits just as much as obsolete products, poor salesmanship or excessive production costs.

During the rapid economic expansion of the postwar years many firms grew without changing their 'organisation clothes'. An organisation that is perfectly suitable for 500 employees can lead to serious organisation bottlenecks and losses due to internal conflicts when the firm reaches 1000 employees and a substantial number of products. The result is that in spite of its size the firm cannot compete successfully with smaller firms. It has become a cumbersome and costly machine. Many medium-sized firms have failed in past years through failing to adapt their organisation to their own growth, and many more have gone into a period of stagnation and falling profits for the same reason.

Organisation planning is therefore an important part of company planning. Its purpose is to create the right organisation for achieving the company's

Organisation of a small firm

objectives. An increase in the number of products and markets brings changes in the things the firm has to do and in their relative importance. An organisation is not a static structure, but is for the most part the consequence of historical developments, personal circumstances and the needs of the firm and the market.

If a firm has a single product group and only one market, organisation raises no special problems. The greater the number of products and markets served, the more varied are the demands on the firm. Hence the danger that the old organisation will not be able to cope with market demands that are constantly increasing in complexity.

In small firms in which the main emphasis is on one product, the traditional division into commercial and technical areas is thoroughly effective.

When the demands of the product distribution function increase, the commercial side may be divided into a sales function and a finance and administration function. This development is shown on the next page.

This three-part structure forms a satisfactory basis for further refinement of the organisation, as needed by larger firms with a more diversified product range. Three such organisation structures are described below, all based on a three-part division at top executive level, but with further subdivision of the tasks.

Fig. 13.1   Organisation of a small firm

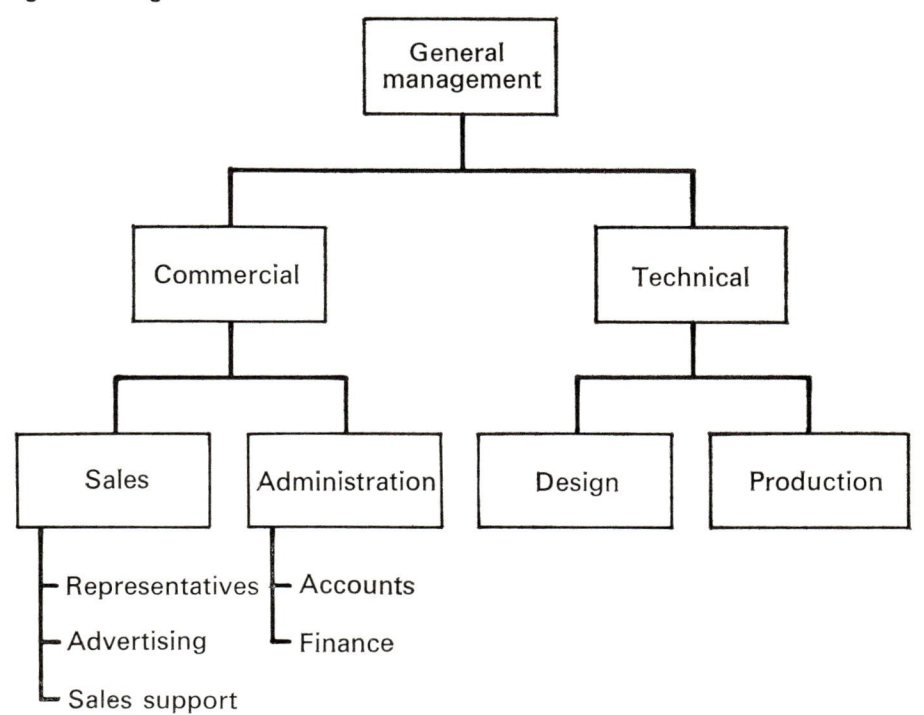

Depending on the relations between products and markets, the following types of firms can be distinguished:

- **The single-product multi-market firm**: A firm of this type only manufactures one product range, but supplies various different market segments.

    For example, a gas company only supplies one product, natural gas, but delivers it to very different customers, such as private users, restaurants, building companies and industrial users. A steel manufacturer has customers as different as the motor car industry, building firms and machinery manufacturers, all of whom he supplies with sheet and sections.
- **The laterally diversified firm**: A firm of this type produces different product ranges for different markets. Particular product ranges can be directly attributed to particular markets.

    For example, a chemical firm may produce synthetic fibres for the textile industry, granules for the plastics industry and fertilisers for agriculture.
- **The multi-product firm**: This produces many products, but sells them through relatively few sales channels. A manufacturer of drugs only supplies wholesalers and hospitals. A food manufacturer may produce soups, sauces, tinned foods and ready-cooked meals, but he only sells to the grocery trade and restaurants.

Fig. 13.2 Organisation of a medium-sized firm

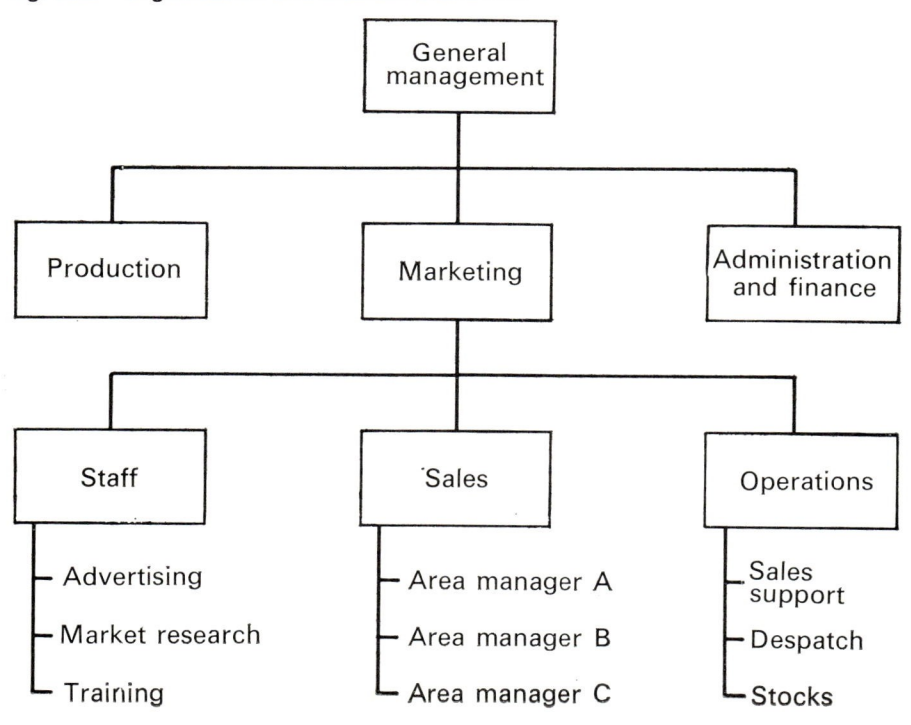

```
                    ┌───────────────────┐
                    │     General       │
                    │    management     │
                    └─────────┬─────────┘
         ┌────────────────────┼────────────────────┐
   ┌─────┴─────┐        ┌─────┴─────┐       ┌──────┴──────────┐
   │Production │        │ Marketing │       │ Administration  │
   │           │        │           │       │  and finance    │
   └───────────┘        └─────┬─────┘       └─────────────────┘
                  ┌───────────┼───────────┐
             ┌────┴───┐  ┌────┴───┐  ┌────┴──────┐
             │ Staff  │  │ Sales  │  │Operations │
             └────┬───┘  └────┬───┘  └────┬──────┘
                  │           │           │
         ─ Advertising   ─ Area manager A   ─ Sales support
         ─ Market research ─ Area manager B ─ Despatch
         ─ Training      ─ Area manager C   ─ Stocks
```

Organisation by market segments

The great majority of firms fall into one or other of these three classes. Hence, the following three basic forms of organisation are of eminently practical importance for organisation planning.

Organisation by market segments

The single-product multi-market firm manufactures only one product, but supplies a large number of different kinds of customer.

The gas company already mentioned does indeed only have one product, but to sell to its various customers effectively it must get adjusted to their various special circumstances and sell through its own specialists. Selling a gas central heating boiler to a private householder involves quite different technical problems, sales arguments, advertising and methods of financing from selling the same boiler to a property developer for installation on a new estate or from selling gas to an industrial firm. It therefore makes sense to have a different sales division for each market. Specialists are then available for each market and the customer is always dealing with somebody he can talk to and who understands his problems. Continued cooperation with the same class of customers facilitates the working out of standard solutions to common problems and increases the effectiveness of the sales effort and technical service.

Fig. 13.3 Organisation by market segments

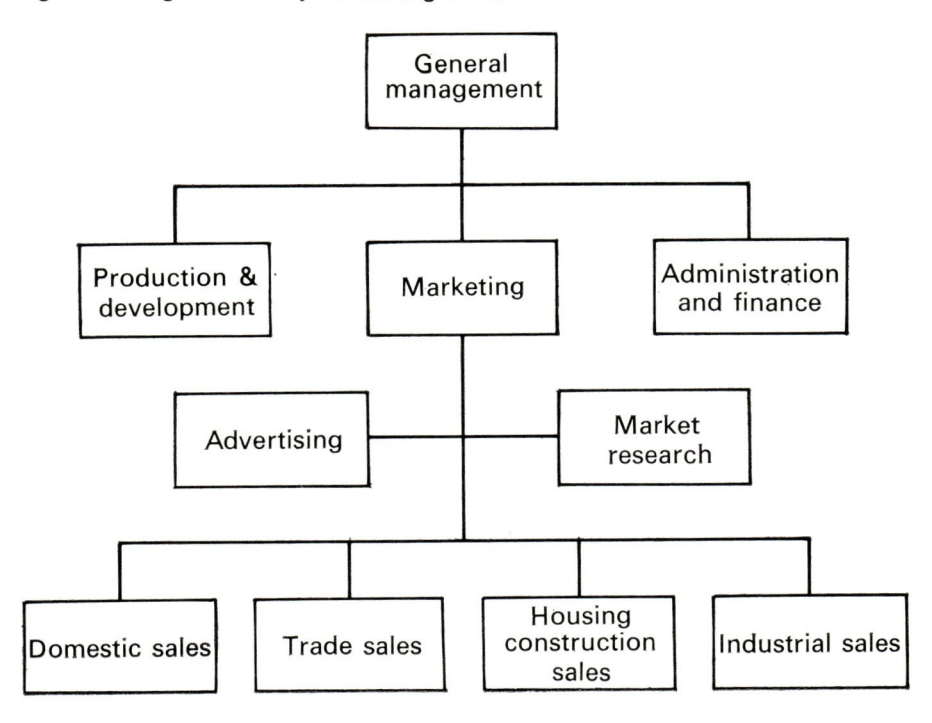

The functions of administration, finance, production, transport and distribution can well be centralised, while sales are organised by market segments. In this way the responsibility for well-directed and intensive attacks on the various markets and accountability for achieving the corresponding sales budgets are clearly regulated. Other instances where single-product sales organisation by market segments makes sense are fuel oil, sheet steel and synthetic materials. The table on the previous page shows organisation by market segments described in terms of the gas industry.

Organisation by operating areas (divisions)

The laterally diversified firm is active in a number of totally separate markets. There is therefore the possibility of dividing not only sales but design and production by areas of operation. They are usually given the title of divisions.

The different divisions then become profit centres, and can be controlled almost as if they were subsidiary companies. Accountability not only for turnover, but for costs and profits can be transferred to the managers of the separate divisions. This form of organisation embraces the advantages of centralisation, namely, coordination of all services in the firm with the advantages of decentralised operations, which are clearly defined responsibilities and short communication paths in the separate divisions.

The headquarters organisation will include finance and administration, as well as the staff functions such as company planning, market research, legal department, personnel department, estates department, and so on.

The managers of the separate divisions are responsible for their profit centres. In practice, they are entrepreneurs and are fully responsible for operating within the budgets authorised by head office. They control sales, expenditure and investment plans. The managers are responsible for the profitability of their divisions, and for the development of new products specific to their area. Diversification planning, that is, planning for new markets or new product groups, is carried out at head office.

Firms that rely on close technical cooperation with their customers are particularly favoured by short communication paths between sales, design and production. Suppliers of components for the motor car industry and the household equipment industry are an example. Other forms of organisation with long communication paths would seriously impede the success of their operations.

Decentralisation is another advantage of organisation by operating areas. Very large firms that are strongly diversified can still be flexible and close to their markets in spite of their size, if they are organised in this way. In recent years, Ruhrstahl, Rheinstahl, Demag, BASF and Bayer have been reorganised on the principle of operating divisions.

A necessary condition for the success of this decentralised form of organisation is an efficient financial and accounting system which takes over the central control function by means of budgets and monthly comparisons between budget

Organisation by product managers

and actual figures for costs, turnover and profit. The following table shows the organisation of a divisionalised firm that operates in the areas of building materials, engineering construction, plastics and packaging materials.

Fig. 13.4 Organisation by operating areas (divisions)

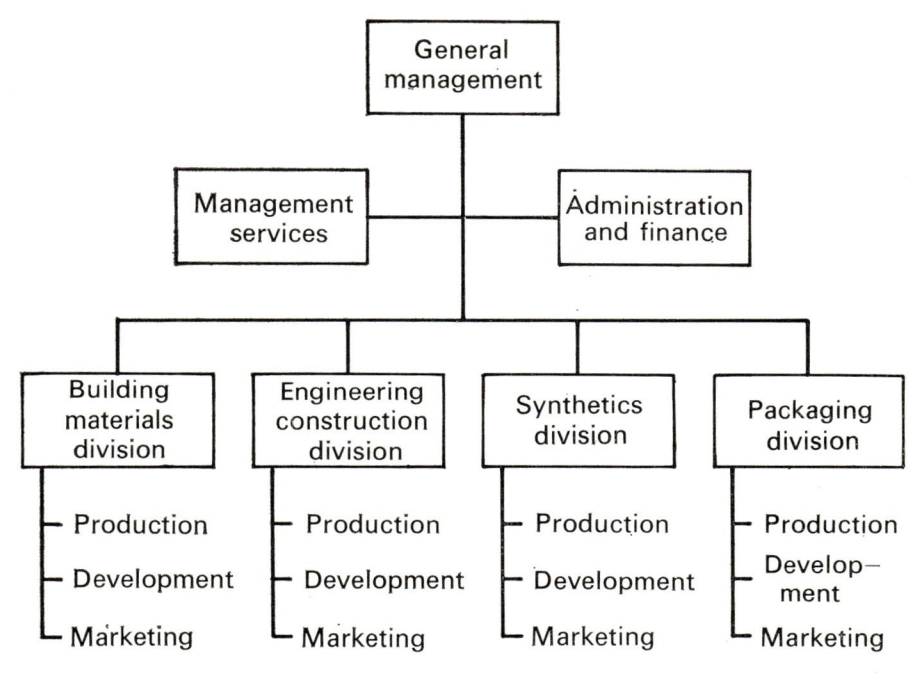

```
                        General
                       management
                           |
        ┌──────────────────┼──────────────────┐
   Management                            Administration
    services                              and finance
                           |
    ┌──────────────┬───────┴───────┬──────────────┐
 Building      Engineering      Synthetics     Packaging
 materials     construction      division       division
 division       division
    |              |                |              |
 ─ Production   ─ Production    ─ Production   ─ Production
 ─ Development  ─ Development   ─ Development  ─ Develop-
 ─ Marketing    ─ Marketing     ─ Marketing      ment
                                               ─ Marketing
```

Organisation by product managers

The multi-product firm is characterised by the fact that individual products cannot be exclusively attributed to particular markets, especially if it has a large number of products that are sold through the same sales channels. The central problem is how to make sure that all the different products get their proper share of the attention and energies of the senior executives. In practice, no single product can command the full attention of the top management. Such firms often operate according to the principle of oiling where it squeaks. The top management plays fire brigades and attends to the current crises. It is too easy to neglect the most important profit-earners and to fail to exploit the full profit or growth potential of particular products.

Organisation by product managers can help to avoid these difficulties. This consists of superimposing on the conventional line organisation by functions and, where appropriate, market segments, a staff organisation with one manager responsible for each product group.

These product managers should have no line duties, and no authority over the line managers responsible for sales, distribution, production or other line functions. The product manager's job is to plan, coordinate and supervise the implementation of plans. He is really more of a diplomat than a manager.

But he is, nevertheless, responsible for the profitability of his product group. This is how his success is measured, and in some firms it affects his annual bonus.

The product manager's tasks include:

- Assembling all the required market information about his products and keeping track of the competition.
- Producing sales forecasts.
- Working out recommendations to the marketing manager for improving turnover and profits, e.g. advertising and sales promotion campaigns, the use of new sales channels, price changes, and so on.
- Keeping track of the measures recommended by him and authorised by the marketing management.

The position of product manager in the firm is difficult and sometimes precarious. He has no line authority: he can only convince, persuade and ask. It is therefore important that all appropriate arrangements should be made in the firm to make his activities as effective as possible. These arrangements include:

- His prestige. He must make up for his lack of executive authority by personal respect and specialised knowledge. A new graduate does not make a successful product manager. The old hands in sales, advertising, etc, will simply not take him seriously.
- Adequate scope. His area of work should not be unnecessarily restricted. He must be in a position to make recommendations relating to all aspects of his products (e.g. advertising, sales promotion, packaging, pricing).
- Direct access to and full support from the marketing management.
- The opportunity to acquire specialised knowledge, e.g. in advertising, market research, etc, in so far as he needs it for the exercise of his duties.
- Clear organisation. The location of responsibilities for sales, market research, advertising, sales training, etc, should be known to all staff and should be observed by them. If an unclear and inexperienced marketing organisation is interfered with by product managers, disasters can happen through individual managers not keeping to the rules of the game. Product managers can easily come to grief in such a situation.

These conditions must exist for a product manager organisation to operate successfully. If it does, it offers substantial **advantages** for the firm as a whole:

- Each individual product receives the undivided attention of a manager who is directly responsible for its success.
- The top management is released from the obligation to intervene on behalf

Organisation with product managers

of individual products. They can devote themselves to their proper tasks such as planning and do not need to act as a fire brigade.
- The profit potential of all the firm's products is better exploited.

The following table shows the organisation of a firm that uses product managers in the food industry.

Fig. 13.5 Organisation with product managers

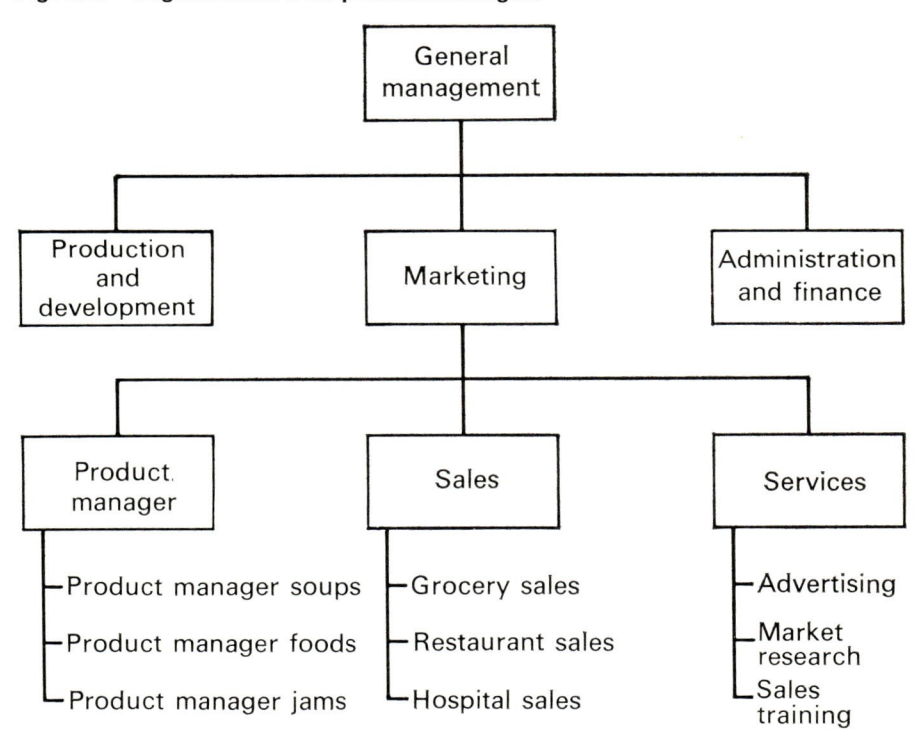

```
                         General
                       management
            ┌──────────────┼──────────────┐
      Production        Marketing     Administration
         and                           and finance
     development
                    ┌─────────┼─────────┐
                Product      Sales     Services
                manager
   ┌─ Product manager soups   ┌─ Grocery sales      ┌─ Advertising
   ├─ Product manager foods   ├─ Restaurant sales   ├─ Market research
   └─ Product manager jams    └─ Hospital sales     └─ Sales training
```

Organisation must be individually designed

The three forms of organisation described in the preceding section represent the basic types of organisation that have justified themselves in practice. There is, however, no ideal organisation. Every organisation structure has to be specially designed to meet the particular needs of the market and the tasks that the firm must carry out to meet these needs. In practice, every organisation also carries the mark of the personal strengths of the managers.

In very large firms, a combination of different organisation structures may be appropriate. A laterally diversified firm can be organised according to the principle of operating areas and also have product managers in particular areas.

Job descriptions

Job descriptions are an effective aid in organisation planning. They state the tasks and responsibilities of the individual managers, but they will only be successful if they are understood and accepted by the managers who hold the positions in question, and also if they are known and accepted by the managers in neighbouring positions. This is the only way of creating the conditions for good cooperation.

The organisation chart shows the system of specialisation and authority, but only the job descriptions show the tasks and responsibilities and the boundaries of the responsibilities of individual managers. They are the basis for cooperation with the minimum of friction. An organisation chart and a set of job descriptions are the two indispensable aids to organisation planning.

14

The organisation of company planning

The following are the conditions for successful and effective planning:

- Creative thinking, to elicit new market strategies and diversification proposals.
- Systematic construction and use of a planning system.
- Sound knowledge of the firm and its markets.
- Entrepreneurial decisions to determine objectives and the choice between different alternatives.
- Coordination of the different parts of the company, in order to implement the plans.

This list makes it clear that no single person or office in the firm is in a position to create all these conditions and to satisfy the many-sided demands.

Hence, company planning can only be carried out successfully if the tasks and responsibilities of a number of people can be suitably coordinated.

Experience shows that the following persons should be involved in company planning:

- The top management.
- The company planning section.
- Line managements, such as sales, production, etc.
- Other services, such as accounts, market research, etc.
- External consultants.

Procuring the necessary information and working out detailed plans should be left as far as possible to the departments immediately concerned, in so far as is within their competence.

Thus, market research can be given the task of investigating the future development of markets, and the marketing departments can be asked to provide forecasts of future turnover, taking into account new products that are already in the planning stage.

The personnel department can provide a survey of the age structure of the firm's employees and its future manpower needs.

It is the task of the company planning section to provide the various departments with the framework for their planning tasks, to support them in the application of planning techniques and to coordinate the various departmental plans.

It is important to involve the firm's managers in the planning process as early and as intensively as possible so that their knowledge and experience can be fully utilised. It also helps to sell the idea of company planning, since the individual managers feel committed if their views have been asked. It helps to prevent the other departments from treating the company planners as long-haired theorists, and not taking their results and action plans seriously. If that happens, company planning is for all practical purposes a dead letter. It is far better to do without a complete and fully integrated plan and to have effective planning, at least in some areas of the company, rather than to draw up a fully integrated plan that stays in someone's drawer.

The Planning Section

Experience has shown that firms with a turnover of about £20 million and upwards need a separate company planning section to take over the detailed work of assembling information, coordinating individual plans and doing the preparatory work for the decisions that have to be taken.

The managers of line departments and other service departments are inevitably so hard-pressed by the daily routine that they cannot help postponing and neglecting the important but less urgent questions of company planning.

The planning manager's tasks are shown in the checklist. As a rule, a company planning section is small, often a one-man section. It is not the number of staff, but the capabilities of the manager that are decisive for its success. It should report directly to the managing director.

The placing of the planning section in the organisation often leads to prestige problems, because the managers of the departments feel that they have been passed over. The consequent tensions do not help the planner.

There is no compelling need to put the company planner above the line department managers in the hierarchy, since he has no authority over them.

But regardless of status and title, the effectiveness of the company planner stands or falls with his being fully switched into the top management information flow. He must participate in all decisions which affect the future position of the company and his views must be heard on the problems that arise.

This can be achieved, for example, by attaching the company planner to the chairman's office as his personal assistant for company planning and development and making him keep the minutes of board meetings.

Checklist 10 The company planner's responsibilities

1 Collecting and evaluating data about the company and its market, such as:
   — Economic developments
   — Technical developments
   — Activity of competitors
   — Technical and economic developments among customers and suppliers
   — Comparisons between company products and the competitors' products
   — Finanacial indices for comparing the company and its competitors
2 Informing the management of the company about current results of evaluations
3 Working out proposals for company objectives
4 Working out and testing proposals for market strategies, extension of the product range, diversification and acquisitions
5 Advising other departments of the company about working out their separate plans
6 Testing proposals and plans put forward by other departments
7 Coordinating the separate plans. Working out an integrated company plan on the basis of the separate plans
8 Working out an action plan as a basis for the annual budget
9 Comparing the annual results with the budget figures in the action plans and the company plan
10 Modifying the company plan to take into account the variances between actual and planned figures

Checklist 11 Common reasons for the failure of company planning

1 Insufficient support from the top management
2 Company planner not reporting directly to the managing director
3 No desire for better results than have been achieved hitherto without company planning
4 Unwillingness of the top management to make long-term decisions
5 Over-hasty declaration of company objectives, without allowing enough time for thought, discussion and maturing of ideas
6 Top management not finding enough time to do the preparatory work for important decisions
7 Insufficient support from other departments, with lack of access to important internal information
8 Insufficient appreciation of the value of company planning
9 Insufficient technical qualifications and inadequate personal qualities of the company planning staff
10 Lack of willingness to use the action plan as a basis for the annual budget

The planning committee

The company planners must have extensive practical business experience. He will often have to use his personal authority in place of the line authority that he does not possess. Hence, it is not sensible to give the job of company planning to a young graduate without practical experience.

A checklist of things that can go wrong with company planning is shown on the previous page.

The planning committee

The formation of a planning committee has been shown by experience to be a suitable way of ensuring the coordination of the various line and staff departments of the firm, and of assuring the managers that their views will be heard when plans are in preparation.

The committee meets between six and ten times a year. Interim planning results and the proposals from individual managers are discussed. As the decisive factors in planning normally come from the market, it makes sense to have the marketing director as chairman of the committee.

The membership may thus include:

- Marketing director (chairman).
- The chief accountant.
- The marketing manager.
- The sales manager.
- The design and development manager.
- The production manager.
- The personnel manager.
- The market research manager.
- The company planner.

Company planning is of prime importance for the future of the company. The top management must be prepared to take it seriously and to devote enough time and energy to the entrepreneurial planning decisions. The company planning manager can help by preparing the information needed for decisions and clarifying the problems on which decisions are needed. But decisions are a matter for the top management, not for the planning manager or the planning committee.

The most important decisions are those relating to the determination of company objectives, the choice of the most suitable market strategies and diversification plans to implement the objectives, and questions of how to finance them. These are decisions that cannot be delegated.

The tasks of the management consultant

An external adviser can be of considerable help to a company that is introducing or developing company planning. In large firms, it is often worth while to use the services of an independent consultant with appropriate knowledge and experience when company planning is being installed. Small- and medium-sized firms may find it advisable to dispense with a planning section of their own and to employ a consultant to assemble information, coordinate plans and prepare the decisions.

A checklist for the tasks that can be performed with advantage to the company by an independent consultant follows.

The timescale for the introduction of company planning

From the time of its introduction to the time when it produces its first useful results, company planning takes, in practice, at least three years.

Working out the planning tasks, carrying out the company appraisal and deciding on company objectives usually takes at least one year.

Only then can work begin on plans for market strategies and action plans. And not until the first comparisons between planned and actual figures have been made and the consequences drawn, does the company begin to feel the first practical effects of planning on profits.

In order to shorten this set-up time and to gain experience of operating simple planning systems, it may be advisable to begin with open planning in the areas of marketing and finance, and not to bring other areas, such as production and manpower, into the planning system until later. Afterwards, the separate plans can be integrated into a comprehensive company plan.

The path is long and difficult. It needs courage, persistence and energy.

But the company planner should always remember the Chinese proverb: 'Even the longest journey begins with a first step.'

Checklist 12 The planning consultant's brief

1 To introduce company planning in respect of tasks, methods, responsibilities and organisation.
2 To advise the top management about the preparatory work needed for decisions about company objectives and strategies for achieving them.
3 To examine critically and evaluate proposals and plans worked out by the company planner.
4 To assemble data and carry out market research on new product proposals.
5 To work out marketing plans and strategies.
6 To evaluate other firms proposed as acquisitions.
7 To integrate the separate plans into a company plan.
8 To work out action plans as a basis for annual budgets.
9 To advise the various departments of the company on their separate plans.
10 To be a member of the Planning Committee.

Appendix:
The Checklists

Checklist 1 The process of integrated company planning

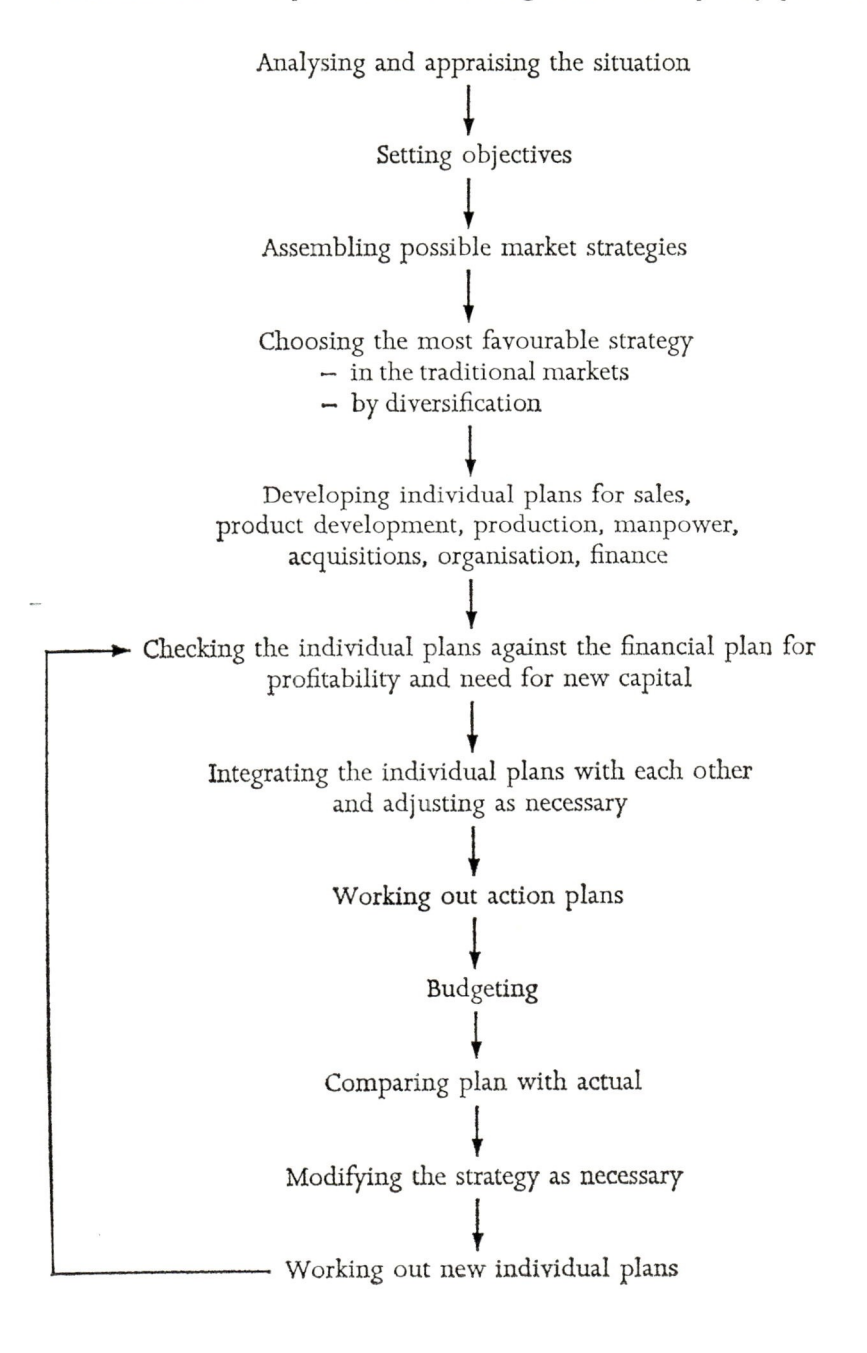

Analysing and appraising the situation
↓
Setting objectives
↓
Assembling possible market strategies
↓
Choosing the most favourable strategy
– in the traditional markets
– by diversification
↓
Developing individual plans for sales,
product development, production, manpower,
acquisitions, organisation, finance
↓
→ Checking the individual plans against the financial plan for
profitability and need for new capital
↓
Integrating the individual plans with each other
and adjusting as necessary
↓
Working out action plans
↓
Budgeting
↓
Comparing plan with actual
↓
Modifying the strategy as necessary
↓
Working out new individual plans

Checklist 2 The company appraisal

Part 1 The current situation

The market

1 In which markets do our products have a part to play?

2 How big is the total market?

— Home, Common Market, Europe, overseas.

3 What is the share of the separate market segments?

— By the nature, age, size, etc, of the user.
— By the nature of the demand (first purchase, replacement purchase).
— By sales channels.

4 What important factors influence the customers' decision to select this brand of product?

— Technical properties, performance, capacity.
— Shape, colour, styling.
— Sales density, customer service.
— Price, discount, trading terms.
— Manufacturer's reputation (image).

The firm

1 What is the firm's share of the market now?

— In total – home – Common Market – Europe.
— In the individual market segments.

2 What is the customers' appraisal of our products?

3 How good is our performance, taking, account of brand selection criteria and future requirements?

4 Where are the strengths and weaknesses of our firm in respect of manpower, finance, products, product development, production technology, sales?

The competitors

1 What are their market shares?

— Home – Common Market – Europe.
— In the individual market segments.

2 What is the customers' appraisal of their products?

3 What are the strengths and weaknesses of the most important competitors in respect of finance, products, product development, production technology sales?

Checklist 2 The company appraisal

Part 2 Future developments

The market

1 How will the requirements and habits of the customers change in the future?

— Technical requirements on the product.
— Sales channels.
— Customer service.

2 How will the demand develop?

— Home – Common Market – Europe – Overseas.
— By the nature, age, size, etc, of the consumers.
— By the nature of the demand (first or subsequent purchase).

3 How will prices and margins develop?

4 How will the composition of the customers change in the future?

5 Will new suppliers enter the market?

The firm and its future opportunities

1 What market shares can we expect in the future if we continue on our present course?

2 What future market share can we expect if:

— The products are modernised?
— The product range is extended?
— The sales effort is intensified?

3 What changes in sales strategy are possible, in order to increase turnover?

— New sales channels.
— Attacking certain market segments more strongly.
— Better direction of the sales force.

4 What resources will be needed for such changes, in respect of manpower, development, capital?

5 Will the financial resources be sufficient?

6 Will specialists be needed? Of what level? How many?

7 What organisation changes will be needed in the firm or in the sales division?

Checklist 3 Quantitative planning objectives

Turnover
— Increase in total turnover
— Increase in turnover in particular market segments

Returns
— Increase in profits before tax
— Increase in contribution to overheads
— Improvement in return on capital
— Increase in profit after tax
— Improvement in return on turnover

Finance
— Reduction in debtors as percentage of turnover
— Reduction in the period of outstanding claims
— Reduction in short-term obligations
— Improvement in the ratio of internal to external capital

Production
— Increase in contribution per employee
— Reduction of waste as a percentage of production
— Reduction in the ratio of customer complaints to sales
— Reduction in the ratio of warranty work to sales
— Reduction of late deliveries

Stock control
— Reduction in the value of stocks (finished goods, raw materials, work in progress) in relation to sales

Manpower
— Improvement in the rate of turnover
— Achievement of a specified number of employees

Advertising
— Improvement in the degree of knowledge of the firm by the relevant consumer groups

Sales
— Distribution density
— Number of prospects called upon
— Number of new customers
— Sales costs as a percentage of turnover
— Cost of the sales force as percentage of turnover
— Number of customer inquiries
— Number of offers sent out
— Ratio of offers to orders

Checklist 4 Rationalisation methods

Production
— Materials flow in production
— Value analysis of the products
— Method improvements
— Larger batch sizes
— Buying parts in, instead of manufacturing them

Distribution
— Too many, or too few, warehouses
— Materials flow in the warehouses
— Methods of dispath (rail, carrier, own transport)
— Changing the routing of products from the factory to the customer

Sales
— Changing the sales channels (wholesalers, agents, representatives)
— More carefully directed activities of the sales force
— Are all prospects known?
— Are they classified according to importance?
— Are the sales journeys planned in relation to the importance of the prospects?
— Rejection of unprofitable orders, order quantities and products
— Extending the product-line

Checklist 5 Market research

1 Who are the potential customers for my products?
  How are they made up:

  — Kind (sex, age, size, industry, etc)?
  — Number, structure?
  — Geographical location?

2 For what purposes is the product used?

3 What criteria are used by the trade and the consumer in selecting the preferred brand or manufacturer?

4 What demands are made by the customer in respect of:

  — Properties (performance, size, shape)?
  — Sales, technical advice, customer service?
  — Lead times?
  — Methods of financing?

5 How will these demands change in the future?

6 What share of the demand goes through the different sales channels? What is the future trend?

7 What is the customers' appraisal of the competitors and their products?

8 What sources of information are used by the customer to inform himself about what is being offered?

9 What shares of the market are held by the most important competitors?

10 What kind of sales organisation do the competitors use?

11 Are the customers currently satisfied with the competitors' products, sales and customer service? What are the possible sources of dissatisfaction?

12 Are there still unsolved problems with the products or the customer service? How strongly are they influencing the selection of brand of manufacture?

13 To what extent are the trade and the consumers willing to stock or use a new make of product? What conditions must be satisfied for them to do so? (Price, discounts, quality, customer service.)

Checklist 6 Market planning

1 How must sales be organised to reach the most interesting segments of the market at an acceptable cost?

— What sales channels can be used?
— What trade margins have to be allowed?
— What kind of a sales force is needed to call on customers and the trade (number, specialist qualifications, training)

2 What has to be done in the area of sales promotion and advertising?

— Advertising: kind, quantity, media
— Sales aids, brochures, display materials, self-service racks, exhibitions
— Training of retailers and sales force
— Technical advice to trade and customer on applications of the product

3 What market shares can be expected from the different sales strategies?

— What are the expected ratios of turnover and costs?

4 How should distribution be organised?

— What time interval between order and delivery does the market demand?
— How many warehouses for products and spare parts are required?
— Where can products and parts be stored? By the retailers? In the firm's own warehouses?
— How should dispatch be organised?

5 What level of performance is expected of customer service and spare part service? How can it be achieved?

— Through the firm's own branches? Through the trade? From the factory?
— What personnel are needed and what costs will be incurred?

6 What are the possible price policies?

— Fixed prices, list prices, free prices?
— What is the price structure for customer service and spares?
— Reductions, discounts, quantity rebates, credit terms?

Checklist 7 Licensing contracts

1 Market research: investigate the sales opportunities for the product and the technical demands of the market before signing the contract: it often happens that technical changes have to be made in the product, to make it suitable for the home market.

2 What the licensor has to provide: patent rights, know-how (design, production, sales), drawings, tools, brand markings, advertising.

3 Duration of the contract and of the payment of royalties; arrangements for terminating the contract.

4 Reduction or cancellation of royalties if a patent or part-patent expires or is declared void.

5 Premature termination of the contract if the product does not sell or is rendered obsolete by technical developments.

6 Defence of patents: who must take the legal action and bear the costs?

7 Product improvements by the licensor: the licensee's rights.

8 Product improvements and improvements in the production process by the licensee: effect on royalties; what development costs are borne by the licensor?

9 Delimitation of licensor's and licensee's markets, rules relating to export and re-export; transfer of existing customers from the licensor to the licensee.

10 Delimitation in respect of other future licensees in other countries. (The EEC rules on cartels make this increasingly difficult.)

11 Issue of licences or know-how to third parties. Issue of sublicences. Cross-licensing agreements with business partners of the licensee. Incorporation of parts or subassemblies made under licence in products other than those envisaged in the agreement.

12 Manufacture or sale of competing products by the licensee.

13 Methods of calculation of royalties and time when they fall due: on production, on being sold, or on reaching an agreed turnover?

14 Evidence and documentation of production, sales or turnover.

15 Quality control by the licensor; agreements about taking samples, approving the production process or the factory.

16 Agreement about legal obligation for the product and defence against customer claims under consumer protection.

17 Deduction of taxes from royalties. Obtaining the necessary currency permits.

18 Defence against cartel legislation. Costs of cartel proceedings. Changes in the agreement if important conditions are disallowed. (Especially important because the EEC market has a rather strong anti-trust legislation which might render sales protection clauses between licensor and licensee void.)

19 Period of protection: embargo on production and sales after the expiration of the contract.

20 Agreement about an arbitrator in case of difficulties.

Checklist 8 Product planning

1. How large is the market for the new product and how is it expected to develop in the future?
2. Who are the competitors?
3. What are the characteristics of the competitors' products?
4. Are the customers currently satisfied with the technical characteristics of the available products?
5. In what direction are the customers' technical demands expected to change?
6. Does the company have proper facilities for selling the product? Can a suitable sales organisation and customer service be built up?
7. What share of the market can the company expect to capture? Is this enough for economical production?
8. By what date at the latest must the new product be available, if the sales targets are to be achieved?
9. What technical and economic characteristics must the product have in order to penetrate the market and to persuade customers to change from the makes they are buying at present? What are the required features of:

    performance, length of useful life, shape, style, colour, reliability purchase price, operating costs, spares, customer service.
10. What is the relative importance of these features in the customers' eyes? What features determine the decision to buy?
11. For what properties are the customers willing to pay a higher price?
12. At what price is the product acceptable to the market?

Checklist 9 The personnel manager's duties

1. Establish the future need for personnel by number and quality of employees on the basis of the manpower plan.
2. Procure job descriptions for all managerial positions.
3. Conduct appointment interviews, evaluate candidates. Make new appointments.
4. Develop and administer a wage and salary structure, including salary brackets for each position and incentive premiums.
5. Introduce and service a system of appraisal of all employees by their superior, as a basis for promotion and planning the filling of vacancies.
6. Identify employees suitable as successors to the present management.
7. Develop and administer internal and external training programmes, so that employees can become familiar with modern methods.
8. Work out individual training programmes (attendance at courses and seminars, job rotation) for managers and future managers worthy of promotion.
9. Administer all personnel records.
10. Organise and administer the social programmes (pension fund, life insurance, medical aid, canteen, sports club, etc).
11. Organise and administer suggestion schemes.
12. Represent the firm in matters relating to works council, trade unions, labour law, accident prevention.
13. Observe morale in the firm to take steps to keep it as high as possible.
14. Contact with employers' federations and employment officers at universities and colleges.

Limitation of responsibilities: The personnel manager is responsible for ensuring that the firm has at all times the right number and quality of employees. He cannot appoint, dismiss or promote anyone or award any increase in wages or salary without the consent of the functional manager concerned. He cannot make any alterations in the organisation structure of the firm without the consent of the manager concerned.

Checklist 10 The company planner's responsibities

1 Collecting and evaluating data about the company and its market, such as:
   — Economic development
   — Technical development
   — Activity of competitors
   — Technical and economic developments among customers and suppliers
   — Comparisons between company products and the competitors' products
   — Finanacial indices for comparing the company and its competitors

2 Informing the management of the company about current results of evaluations

3 Working out proposals for company objectives

4 Working out and testing proposals for market strategies, extension of the product range, diversification and acquisitions

5 Advising other departments of the company about working out their separate plans

6 Testing proposals and plans put forward by other departments

7 Coordinating the separate plans. Working out an integrated company plan on the basis of the separate plans

8 Working out an action plan as a basis for the annual budget

9 Comparing the annual results with the budget figures in the action plans and the company plan

10 Modifying the company plan to take into account the variances between actual and planned figures

Checklist 11 Common reasons for the failure of company planning

1 Insufficient support from the top management
2 Company planner not reporting directly to the managing director.
3 No desire for better results than have been achieved hitherto without company planning.
4 Unwillingness of the top management to make long-term decisions.
5 Over-hasty declaration of company objectives, without allowing enough time for thought, discussion and maturing of ideas.
6 Top management not finding enough time to do the preparatory work for important decisions.
7 Insufficient support from other departments, with lack of access to important internal information.
8 Insufficient appreciation of the value of company planning.
9 Insufficient technical qualifications and inadequate personal qualities of the company planning staff.
10 Lack of willingness to use the action plan as a basis for the annual budget.

Checklist 12 The planning consultant's brief

1 To introduce company planning in respect of tasks, methods, responsibilities and organisation.
2 To advise the top management about the preparatory work needed for decisions about company objectives and strategies for achieving them.
3 To examine critically and evaluate proposals and plans worked out by the company planner.
4 To assemble data and carry out market research on new product proposals.
5 To work out marketing plans and strategies.
6 To evaluate other firms proposed as acquisitions.
7 To integrate the separate plans into a company plan.
8 To work out action plans as a basis for annual budgets.
9 To advise the various departments of the company on their separate plans.
10 To be a member of the Planning Committee.

Index of Names and Products

AEG, 21, 22, 24, 31, 73, 86
Air-conditioners, 22, 56, 67
ALLGÄUER ALPENMILCH, 55
AVIS, 59, 60

BABCOCK & WILCOX, 32, 58
BAHLSEN, 83
BASF, 57, 72, 74, 77, 114
BAYER, 42, 57, 72, 86, 114
BENDIX, 18
BERTELSMANN, 55
Bicycles, 20
BOHLER & WEBER, 58
Boilers, 18, 58
BOSCH, 18, 21, 22, 24
BROWN-BOVERI, 21, 24
BULL, 31
Burners, 18
BURNHAM, W. H., 30

Carburettors, 18
Cement, 20, 21, 79, 80
Chemicals, 30 , 57, 82, 112
Chocolate, 20
Cigarettes, 23, 42
Coal, 17, 18, 94
Coffee, 20
Computers, 31
CONCORDE, 32, 65
CONSTRUCTOR, 22

Container ships, 22
Cork, 18
Cyclamates, 23

DE GAULLE, 31
DELCHI, 22
DEMAG, 114
DIY, 21
Dow, 77
Dupont, 72

EASTMAN KODAK, 86

Fashion-wear, 6, 16
FENDT, 24
Furniture, 38, 41

Gas, 18, 94, 112, 113
GENERAL ELECTRIC, 21, 31, 72, 86
GENERAL MOTORS, 86
Glass fibre fabrics, 56
GRETSCH, 55
Grocery, 6, 19, 41, 66, 112

HAGELSTEIN, 84
HAKLE, 42
HARRODS, 16
HENKEL, 23
HOECHST, 57, 72
HOHMANN, 74
HONEYWELL, 86

HORTEN, 85

IGNIS, 22
Integrated circuits, 21
INTERNATIONAL HARVESTER, 24
ITT, 27, 59, 91

J. ECKES, 66
JOHN DEERE, 24
JOHN LEWIS, 16
JUNGHEINRICH, 55

KENNEDY, J. F., 29
KOEHRING, 72, 84
KUBA-IMPERIAL, 72

LEAR, 95
LINDE, 21

Machine tools, 16, 63
MASSEY-FERGUSON, 24
MAYTAG, 74
MELITTA, 83
METZELER, 84
MIELE, 24
Mining machinery, 18, 19
Motor cars, 42
Motor cycles, 20, 23

NSU, 95
Nuclear Power, 18, 32

Oil, 17, 18

PALMOLIVE, 23
Paper products, 57
Pesticides, 19
PHILIPS, 21, 31, 45
PHRIX, 77

PINTSCH-BAMAG, 76
PROCTOR & GAMBLE, 23, 30

Radio receivers, 42
RCA, 31
Refrigerators, 18, 21
RHEINSTAHL, 84, 114
RICHTER, 38
RIELLO, 22
ROLLS-ROYCE, 32
RUCKERTSHAUSEN, 56
RUHRSTAHL, 114

SCHWABISCHE HUTTENWERKE, 57
SELFRIDGES, 16
SHERATON HOTELS, 59
SIEMENS, 21, 22, 24, 31, 83, 86
SOLEX, 18
Steel, 57
SUNLIGHT, 23

THYSSEN-BORNEMISZA, 76
Tiles, 22
Toiletries, 20, 41
Tractors, 19, 24, 42, 56
Tyres, 41

UNILEVER, 55

VAN HOUTEN, 20
VOLKSWAGEN, 18, 42, 86, 95
VON BRAUN, W., 29

WALDHOF, 57
Washing machines, 15, 22, 24, 74
Washing powders, 23, 31, 42, 55, 82
WESTINGHOUSE, 21, 31

ZANUSSI, 22